WHAT DID THE ANCIENT ISRAELITES EAT?

WHAT DID THE ANCIENT ISRAELITES EAT?

Diet in Biblical Times

Nathan MacDonald

WILLIAM B. EERDMANS PUBLISHING COMPANY

GRAND RAPIDS, MICHIGAN

Published 2008 by

Wm. B. Eerdmans Publishing Co.

2140 Oak Industrial Drive N.E., Grand Rapids, Michigan 49505

Printed in the United States of America

13 12 11 10 09 08   7 6 5 4 3 2 1

Library of Congress Cataloging-in-Publication Data

MacDonald, Nathan, 1975-

   What did the ancient Israelites eat? Diet in biblical times /
   Nathan MacDonald.

     p.   cm.

   Includes bibliographical references and indexes.

   ISBN 978-0-8028-6298-3 (pbk.: alk. paper)

   1. Food in the Bible. 2. Food — Religious aspects —
   Judaism. 3. Jews — Dietary laws. 4. Bible. O.T. —
   Criticism, interpretation, etc.   I. Title.

BS680.F6M33   2008

221.8'6413 — dc22

                           2008012451

www.eerdmans.com

For my siblings:

Joel, Naomi, Hannah, Esther, Jethro, Miriam and Aaron

Contents

Preface

As surprising as it may seem, this book was written by accident. It began as a brief introductory chapter to a book on some of the ways food is used as a symbol in the Old Testament (since published as *Not Bread Alone: The Uses of Food in the Old Testament* [Oxford: Oxford University Press, 2008]). The purpose of this chapter was to set out what we can know about the Israelite diet from the Old Testament and archaeological sources as necessary background for the interpretative work on the Old Testament. To familiarize myself with the archaeological material, I spent the summer of 2005 in Jerusalem working in the wonderful libraries of the Hebrew University, the Israeli Antiquities Authority, the Albright Institute, and the Centre for British Research in the Levant and meeting Israeli archaeologists and scholars such as Profs. Amnon Ben-Tor, Israel Finkelstein, Amihai Mazar, Mordechai Kislev, Patricia Smith, and Mr. Baruch Rosen. At the end of the summer I discovered that what I had written was far larger than an introductory chapter and too big for a journal.

I shelved what I had written for quite some time, not only because I had a book to write, but also because I was unsure of what to do with it. It seemed to me that, since I am not an archaeologist nor the son of an archaeologist, it was not my book to write, and I had no intentions of writing a second book on food in the Old Testament. As a couple of years passed, I did not become an archaeologist, but I realized that the material I had written touched on so many different areas of knowledge — Old Testament interpretation, Palestinian archaeology, social-scientific approaches, paleopathology — that not only was I not equal to the task, but neither was anyone else. With other scholars, I could claim that I had expertise in one area but was little more than an interested amateur in the others. As a result I was no less qualified than anyone else, and it was therefore not inappropriate or too incautious to publish what I had discovered during my research, so long as the reader was not left in doubt as to my abilities and expertise.

Because the areas of archaeology and gastronomy enjoy wide public interest, I have sought as far as possible to make this book accessible to the general public. Nevertheless, I recognize that many scholars — and probably many who are not — will wish to know the basis for my arguments and observations. As a result I have provided rather substantial notes, but have placed them at the end of the book so as not to distract the reader who has little interest in them. For similar reasons Hebrew words have been transliterated with a very simple system that uses only Latin characters. Those who know Hebrew will readily recognize what words they are when they encounter them. Biblical translations are my own, with the translations of other ancient sources acknowledged in the notes.

I am grateful to the Carnegie Trust for the Universities of Scotland, who funded my time in Jerusalem with a generous grant, and to St. Mary's College for funding the travel to Israel. The Kenyon Institute provided a pleasant base for my time in Jerusalem; the staff and fellow researchers made my time there rewarding and kept me going with various queries and suggestions. I have already mentioned the Israeli scholars I met during my time in Israel, and I am especially grateful to them for the time they gave to someone who was not only a junior scholar, but also a novice in their fields. I am grateful to those who read the entire manuscript and made a number of helpful observations: my father, and Tim and Rachel Stone. I am also indebted to Seth Tarres for indexing the book. My colleagues in St. Andrews University have provided a steady stream of teasing whenever I have discussed my chosen area of research, and the members of my local congregation, Cupar Baptist Church, have regularly asked how my "recipe book" is progressing. I am grateful to them all for the concern they have shown for my growth in humility! Finally, I am deeply indebted to my wife, who has given me the necessary space and time to research, has encouraged me when I needed it and cajoled me when the promised two books had not yet appeared.

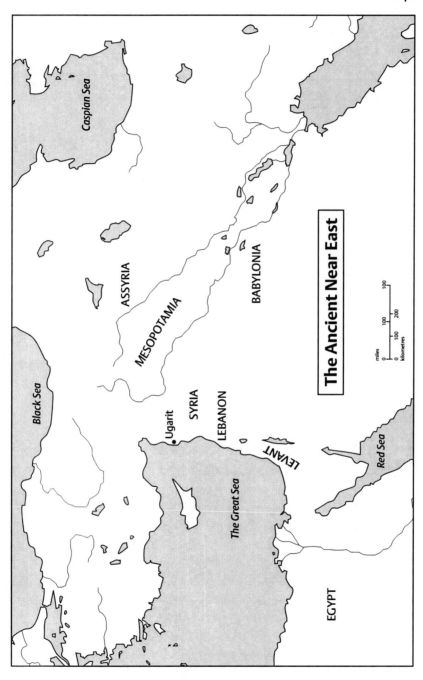

The Ancient Near East

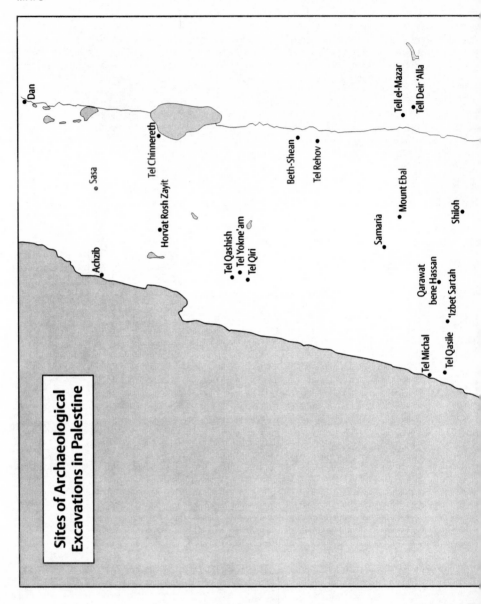

Sites of Archaeological
Excavations in Palestine

Dan

Sasa

Tel Chinnereth

Horvat Rosh Zayit

Achzib

Tel Qashish
Tel Yokne'am
Tel Qiri

Beth-Shean

Tel Rehov

Samaria

Mount Ebal

Shiloh

Tell el-Mazar
Tell Deir 'Alla

Qarawat
bene Hassan
'Izbet Sartah

Tel Michal
Tel Qasile

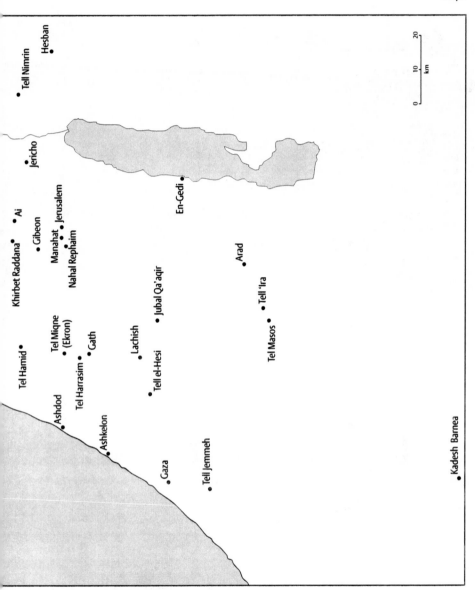

Hesban

Tell Nimrin

Jericho

Ai

Khirbet Raddana

Gibeon

Manahat

Jerusalem

Nahal Rephaim

En-Gedi

Arad

Jubal Qaʾaqir

Tel Hamid

Tel Miqne
(Ekron)

Gath

Lachish

Tell ʿIra

Tell el-Hesi

Tel Masos

Tel Harrasim

Ashdod

Ashkelon

Gaza

Tell Jemmeh

Kadesh Barnea

0   10   20
km

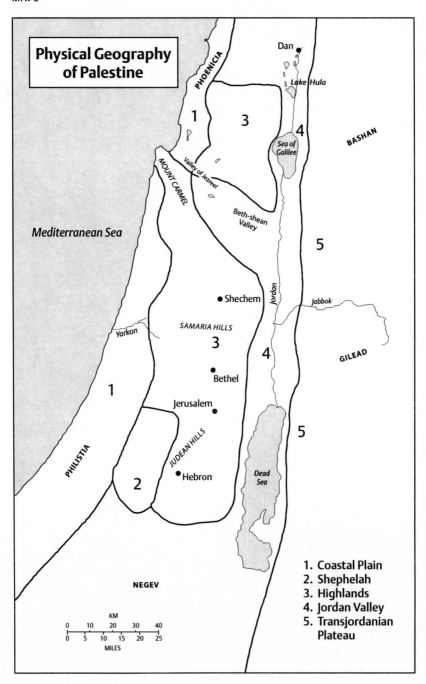

**Physical Geography
of Palestine**

PHOENICIA

Dan

Lake Hula

1

3

4

Sea of
Galilee

BASHAN

MOUNT CARMEL

Valley of Jezreel

Beth-shean
Valley

5

Mediterranean Sea

Shechem

Jordan

Jabbok

SAMARIA HILLS

Yarkon

3

4

GILEAD

1

Bethel

Jerusalem

5

JUDEAN HILLS

PHILISTIA

2

Hebron

Dead
Sea

1. Coastal Plain
2. Shephelah
3. Highlands
4. Jordan Valley
5. Transjordanian
   Plateau

NEGEV

KM
0   10   20   30   40
0   5   10   15   20   25
MILES

Archaeological Time Line

PERIOD	DATE	TRADITIONAL DESIGNATION
Neolithic	8000-5000 B.C.	
Chalcolithic	5000-3300	
Early Bronze Age	3300-2000	
Middle Bronze Age	2000-1500	
Late Bronze Age	1500-1200	Canaanite Period
Iron Age I	1200-1000	Time of the Judges
Iron Age II	1000-586	Time of the Monarchies
Iron Age III	586-539	The Babylonian Exile
Persian	539-332	
Hellenistic	332-37	
Roman	37 B.C.–A.D. 324	
Byzantine	324-638	

INTRODUCTION

This section begins with an examination of biblical descriptions of the land of Israel and the Israelite diet. These descriptions have influenced not only early Christian and Jewish writers, but also some modern scholars. Despite this, the biblical descriptions need to be read with a little critical distance and examined within the contexts of ancient rhetoric and theology (chapter 1). Since we cannot rely on the biblical descriptions alone in reconstructing the Israelite diet, we consider other possible sources of knowledge about it. Each of these sources requires certain methods and raises specific issues that need to be kept in mind as we use them (chapter 2).

CHAPTER 1

A Land Flowing with Milk and Honey

When God called Moses to lead the oppressed Hebrew slaves from bondage in Egypt to freedom, he promised to bring them into a new land of their own. This land is not explicitly identified; rather it is described in a most memorable way as "a land flowing with milk and honey" (Exod. 3:8, 17). In the desert wanderings that follow the exodus from Egypt, the words of this promise occur again and again. It nourishes the hopes of this landless people while their physical bodies are sustained by the daily supply of manna. When the people come within striking distance of cultivated land and send forth spies to ascertain the strength of the present inhabitants, there is no mismatch between expectation and reality. The spies return laden with fruit and the assurance that the land they saw does indeed flow with milk and honey (Num. 13:27). For the prophet Ezekiel sitting in exile in Babylonia, these descriptions are not superlative enough. According to him, it is not only a land flowing with milk and honey, it is also "the most glorious of all lands" (Ezek. 20:15).

The book of Deuteronomy, which is set immediately before the crossing of the river Jordan, is particularly fond of the expression "land flowing with milk and honey," and that is where this vision of the land makes its fullest imprint. Not only does this classic description of the land appear more frequently there than in any other biblical book, but the flowing rhetoric of Deuteronomy finds many other ways of describing the agricultural abundance that is almost within the people's grasp. In one instance Moses gives a catalogue of the land's bounty that incorporates a suggestion of mineral wealth as well as agricultural richness: "YHWH your God is bringing you into a good land, a land with flowing streams, with springs and underground waters welling up in valleys and hills, a land of wheat and barley, of vines and fig trees and pomegranates, a land of olive trees and honey, a land where you may eat bread without scarcity, where you will lack nothing, a land whose stones are iron and from whose hills you may mine copper. You shall eat your fill and bless YHWH your God for the good land that he has given you" (Deut. 8:7-10). On other occasions Deuteronomy refers to the land's abundant fertility with the Mediterranean triad of grain, wine, and olive oil. There are common words for these in Hebrew, but these are abandoned in favor of an archaic and poetic nomenclature — *dagan, tirosh, yitshor.*

It is not surprising that subsequent Jewish and Christian writers were influenced by the biblical characterization of the Promised Land. In the first century A.D. the Jewish historian Josephus waxed lyrical about Palestine:

> Both regions [Judea and Samaria] consist of hills and plains, yield a light and fertile soil for agriculture, are well wooded and abound in fruits, both wild and cultivated; both owe their productiveness to the entire absence of dry deserts and to a rainfall for the most part abundant. All the running water has a singularly sweet taste; and owing to the abundance of excellent grass the cattle yield more milk than in other districts. But the surest testimony to the virtues and thriving condition of the two countries is that both have a dense population.[1]

The Christian ecclesiastical historian Hegesippus takes up Josephus's description:

> The land is rich and grassy: it is adorned with every kind of crop, and dotted with trees. Indeed it would charm any one, and would attract even a lazy man to think about working on the land. . . . The ground is easy to work with implements, and fairly soft, which makes it good for corn, and second to none for its fertility, I should say. Certainly it is the best as far as ripening is concerned, for they are already harvesting there while in other places they are still sowing. No place produces corn of a more excellent quality or appearance. . . . The region is wooded, and thus rich in cattle, flowing with milk, and there is positively no other place where cows have udders so full of milk. Fruit, whether wild or cultivated, is more abundant in this region than in any other.[2]

Some of Hegesippus's additional flourishes are clearly inspired by the biblical text. The prophet Amos's future vision of plowman and reaper overtaking one another has become reality and not only is the milk of the cattle abundant, but the land can truly be said to flow with it. From Hegesippus the description of the land's bounty went on to influence Eucherius in the fifth century and, to a lesser extent, Bede.[3] Many Christian writers obtained their knowledge of Palestine from books, but not all of them. In an account of his pilgrimage to the Holy Land in A.D. 570, the anonymous Piacenza pilgrim described Galilee as "a paradise with corn and fruit like Egypt. The region is small, but in its wine, oil and apples it is superior to Egypt. The millet is abnormally tall, and the stalks are bigger than the height of a man."[4] The reason for God's decision to settle the chosen people in the land of Israel could not be clearer.

It is hardly surprising that ancient Israelite and Jewish writers spoke of their homeland in exalted terms. Rarely did they have any experience of other lands, and when they did, some of Israel's neighbors would have provided a favorable comparison. The rocky and arid hills of Edom, or the deserts of Sinai and Egypt, make Israel look like a veritable paradise.[5] Indeed, in the tale of Sinuhe Palestine appears particularly fertile when seen through Egyptian eyes. This tale from the Middle Egyptian period (early second millennium B.C.) provides a description of Palestine or, as it calls it, the land of Yaa: "It was a good land called Yaa. Figs were in it and grapes. It had more wine than water. Abundant was its honey, plentiful its oil. All kind of fruit were on its trees. Barley was there and emmer, and no end of cattle of all kinds."[6] Still more influential on Jewish writers was the conviction that the land had been given by God to the patriarchs, and could hardly be less than very good. Christian writers, on the other hand, often did not have firsthand experience of Palestine and frequently derived their knowledge of the area from other literary sources. For them the abundance of the Promised Land confirmed the generosity of God and promised a more exalted spiritual inheritance to the church.

The biblical portrayal has also proved influential for modern scholars working on the agriculture of ancient Israel and the diet of its inhabitants. Oded Borowski, for example, begins his book-length treatment of Israelite agriculture with the biblical descriptions of the land, which he affirms as basically accurate, if slightly idealized. "Eretz Israel was regarded by the OT as 'a land flowing with milk and honey' (Exod 3:8). A more detailed description of its agricultural richness and mineral resources is presented to the Israelites with the words [of Deut. 8:7-9]. . . . Although some of the details in this description are idealized, the portrayal of the agricultural versatility of Palestine is accurate."[7] The accuracy of the biblical account is "evident from historical documents and archaeological discoveries." The description of the "land of Yaa" in the tale of Sinuhe is the parade example of the former, and Borowski observes the happy coincidence of overlap between its description of Palestine and that of Deuteronomy 8. According to Borowski, there are good grounds for emphasizing Palestine's agricultural versatility and diversity.

Borowski is similarly optimistic in his assessment of the diet of the ancient Israelites. In an account of daily life in biblical times, he writes, "It is assumed that the ancient Mediterranean diet was a healthy one, and many modern references are made to this effect. Although there is evidence that some of the ancient inhabitants of the region were not slim and trim, most of the available information suggests that most people were not overweight, due to their diet and the strenuous physical activities in which they were engaged."[8] Borowski equates the ancient Israelite diet with the modern Mediterranean diet with its well-known health benefits and clearly assumes that the principal dietary threat to the ancient Israelites was overeating and obesity. In his view, some of the inhabitants were overweight, but most were slim and trim. The exertions associated with farming account for some of this physical well-being, but credit must also be given to the diversity and goodness of their diet. This diversity can be appreciated by listing foods known to have been available to the ancient Israelites either because they are mentioned in the biblical texts or have been found in archaeological excavations. Borowski lists and discusses various grains, pulses, vegetables, fruits, nuts, meats, and dairy products. The same approach is found in King and Stager's introduction to life in ancient Israel. Again the biblical accounts of the land's fecundity, corroborated by Egyptian evidence, form the perspective for considering the production and consumption of food in ancient Israel. The diversity of the land's produce is demonstrated with an extensive list of foodstuffs that contributed to the Israelite diet.[9]

The combination of biblical texts, other texts from the ancient world, and modern scholarly works makes for impressive testimony to the agricultural bounty of ancient Palestine and the healthiness of the ancient Israelite diet. It may appear somewhat churlish to question whether this is the whole truth or even part of it, but it is necessary if we want an accurate assessment of the ancient Israelite diet. Let us make some critical observations on the statements that have been made.

First, we should give careful attention to the Bible's lyrical descriptions of the land. The most influential is of course the description of Palestine as a "land flowing with milk and honey." There is some dispute over the exact meaning of parts of the expression. The term for milk *(chalab)* could easily be the word for "fat" *(cheleb)*, and the word for honey *(debash)* could indicate not bees' honey but a sweet syrup made from fruit.[10] However the expression is understood, it seems to evoke a general sense of the bounty of the land.[11] Certainly this seems to be how it is used in Numbers 13 when the spies return from scouting out the land. Although they come bearing grapes, figs, and pomegranates, they describe the land with the stereotypical expression "a land flowing with milk and honey."[12] The expression suggests an ecological richness that can be exhibited in a number of different ways, not only with milk and honey.

Nevertheless, the use of this expression in the biblical texts is noteworthy, for it is distributed in a rather distinctive manner through the Old Testament.[13] The majority of occurrences are in the Pentateuch,[14] and when the expression occurs in the Prophets or later writings, it always refers back to the promise given to the patriarchs or the people in the wilderness.[15] In other words, the expression is always used to describe a land that the people of Israel have not yet experienced.[16] This is especially apparent when we consider the final use of the expression in Israel's historical writings. In Joshua 5 the people of Israel eventually enter the land after forty years of wandering in the wilderness, and we are given one final reminder of the promise to bring the people into "a land flowing with milk and honey" (v. 6). When the people begin their entry into the land, the manna suddenly ceases and they begin to eat from the fruit of the land. But the reality of life in the land is far more prosaic than the promise suggested, for rather than milk and honey, their first meal in the land is the rather bland "unleavened cakes and parched grain" (v. 11). Thus, we might say that in the Old Testament the land flowing with milk and honey is always a future expectation, or to echo the writer of the New Testament book of Hebrews, "a land flowing with milk and honey still remains for the people of God."[17]

In the description of the land in Deuteronomy 8 we encounter a different set of problems. The language is again lyrical and Palestine is described as a paradise where the people will lack nothing. But does it describe the reality of Israelite experience? Our suspicions might be aroused by the description of Palestine as a land with hills full of iron and copper (v. 9), for the nearest mines are in Transjordan or the Arabah.[18] If Deuteronomy 8 is somewhat generous in its account of Israel's mineral deposits, might not this also be true of its agricultural wealth? We may conclude, then, that many of the biblical expressions about the land have a particular rhetorical and theological purpose. Only with care and with some qualification can they be used to understand the actual experience of the land by the ancient Israelites.

Second, Borowski considers the ancient Israelite diet part of a general Mediterranean diet. He has good grounds for doing so. Israel shares many geographical and climatic features with other areas that border the Mediterranean Sea. It has a temperate winter climate with good rainfall during which crops can be grown and a hot, dry summer. On its hills vines and olives can be grown, and in its valleys wheat and barley. The mainstays of the Israelite diet are the so-called Mediterranean triad of bread, wine, and olive oil.

The virtues of the Mediterranean diet have been widely publicized in recent years, especially in contrast to the patterns of consumption common in many other Western societies. The low incidence of heart disease and cancer among the peoples of southern Europe is largely attributed to dietary factors. Since the basic elements of the diet are the Mediterranean triad, which has remained unchanged across the centuries, it is tempting to draw similar conclusions about the ancient Mediterranean diet. However, there are good grounds, as the classical scholar Peter Garnsey has argued, for some hesitancy at this point.[19] For one thing, the Mediterranean diet has not remained static. Tomatoes, potatoes, and many other fruits and vegetables have been introduced over the centuries, and as the diet has diversified, the dominance of the Mediterranean triad has diminished. For ancient periods, then, we must reckon with a diet that was considerably narrower than the modern Mediterranean diet and dominated by cereals. This is not an unimportant observation since it is now widely recognized that only a varied diet will provide all the vitamins and minerals that humans need.

Third, listing the potential foodstuffs available to the Israelites — as Borowski and also King and Stager do — is an exercise vulnerable to serious misunderstanding. On the one hand, it stands in a long academic tradition of responsible lexicography to investigate the meaning of individual Hebrew words. The Old Testament presents a bewildering array of flora and fauna that the Israelites consumed. Many of these items are of uncertain meaning, and by listing them and discussing their possible meanings a valuable service is rendered to the reader of the Bible. But it is also possible to inadvertently be taken up with a rhetorical exercise that far outdoes Deuteronomy 8 as we provide the fullest possible listing of items that could have made it onto the Israelite menu. The impression is easily given that each of the foods listed was available to the average Israelite and potentially contributed to his or her diet. In reality, the weekly menu of the average Israelite covered a narrow range of foods, and many of the items mentioned in the Old Testament may rarely or never have passed the average Israelite's lips. Nor is dietary variation the only issue at stake here. As important was the question of access to food. We cannot assume that every Israelite, especially the very poor, was able to acquire sufficient food for his or her daily nourishment, especially if we include the vagaries of climate, the unequal distribution of goods, and the occurrence of war and famine.

In the pages that follow I will attempt to give a sober and accurate account of the diet of the ancient Israelites. It should already be apparent that this is by no means a straightforward task. It involves a careful, reflective examination of the many biblical texts that speak about food and agriculture, an assessment of the archaeological evidence for food consumption, and much more besides. Therefore, in the next chapter we will consider some of the methodological issues that confront us as we examine the diet of the ancient Israelites.

CHAPTER 2

Reconstructing the Israelite Diet

What food did the ancient Israelites eat, and in what quantities? With these two deceptively simple questions we confront a topic that is complex and multifaceted. To provide answers we must concern ourselves with all the various stages in the food process. Jack Goody has identified these as production, distribution, preparation, consumption, and disposal of food.[1] Clearly we shall not be able to map these five phases exhaustively, perhaps not even sufficiently, but such limitations are characteristic of historical disciplines and the constraints within which historians ordinarily work. What kind of evidence must be taken into account? And just as important, what are the limitations of the evidence? As we have seen in our brief consideration of the works by Borowski and King and Stager, the evidence for the ancient Israelite diet must be carefully weighed and critically assessed.

It is possible to identify five main sorts of evidence that are relevant to the examination of the ancient Israelite diet. These are the biblical text, archaeological data, comparative evidence from the ancient world, comparative evidence from modern anthropological research, and modern scientific knowledge of geography and nutrition. Not only does each area have its own distinct methods and issues, but each also interacts in a complex manner with each of the other areas. Some of these are general issues of interpretation, but some relate particularly to the problem of reconstructing the ancient Israelite diet.

Our first set of sources is the collection of documents known as the Old Testament or the Hebrew Bible. These are by some distance the largest and most important collection of written documents surviving from ancient Israel. At a general level the biblical texts offer a particular challenge to those who wish to use them in any task of historical reconstruction. First, the compositional complexity of the Old Testament books can hardly be overstated. The present text reflects not only oral traditions but also a lengthy process of composition and editing. As a great deal of recent scholarship has emphasized, most of the books in their final form are the result of the activities of a scribal elite based in Jerusalem in the Persian and Hellenistic periods. We should expect the books to bear the impress of their values and judgments, but also to some degree those of their literary predecessors from earlier periods. Second, the biblical books were composed for particular theological, political, and social purposes. They are often uninterested in the matters that most concern modern scholars. On the other hand, when the interests of the biblical authors and scholars overlap, the specific theological purposes of the authors often create a barrier to the questions of the historian. So, for example, the biblical writers' descriptions of historical events frequently do not accord to the canons of modern historical explanation.

The difficulty of using the biblical text for reconstructing the Israelite diet is immediately apparent. At the most fundamental level the Old Testament does not address the questions of diet that we might wish to ask of it. It does not provide an objective, statistical account of the diet of a variety of Israelites from different periods, places, and social groups. When references to food do occur in the Old Testament, they serve the intentions of the authors and editors. In particular, since food is an important symbolic marker, reference to it often indicates more than mere physical sustenance through a particular food item. As we have already seen, milk and honey feature prominently in the descriptions of the Promised Land. Yet, outside of the stereotypical phrase, milk and honey do not appear often in the Old Testament and may not have been important in the diets of most Israelites.

This brings us to another issue: the problem of representation. The frequency with which a foodstuff appears in the Old Testament is no indicator of its frequency within the Israelite diet. In some cases the distribution of foodstuffs probably maps to historical reality. Bread and grain, for example, appear often in the Old Testament and were a significant component of the daily consumption of calories. But other foods are symbolically and rhetorically marked, and so critical reflection is needed to accurately assess their role in the Israelite diet. So, for example, fruit and meat are highly valued, but legumes and vegetables are not. The latter foodstuffs rarely appear in the Old Testament, though they may have appeared frequently at mealtimes. A different kind of problem confronts us in the identification of foods mentioned in the biblical texts. These lexicographical questions frequently demand the use of cognate Semitic languages or the understanding of the word found in the early translations of the Bible. Even with the help of the early translations and languages closely related to Hebrew, such as Arabic, the identification of some foodstuffs remains uncertain.

A second group of sources for reconstructing the Israelite diet is archaeological remains discovered during excavations. These include written documents other than the Old Testament, though they are of a very limited number. The meager epigraphic finds from ancient Palestine do include, however, ostraca from Samaria and Arad, which describe the distribution of flour, bread, wine, and oil.[2] Unlike the Old Testament, these texts do not pose the problem of a complex editorial history. Nevertheless, such material has its own interpretive challenges. The ostraca provide only a limited snapshot of conditions during the Israelite monarchy at one particular point in time, and we may wonder to what extent they are representative of other periods.

There is a vast amount of nonwritten archaeological evidence that provides insight into the diet of the ancient Israelites. A number of the structures that have survived from ancient Israel were used for the production, storage, and preparation of food. Wine and olive presses, storage rooms, and ovens have been found at Iron Age sites throughout Israel. These remains of agricultural installations and storage facilities provide evidence of land use and can give some idea of the level of food production. Food is not only prepared and consumed: that which cannot be digested has to be disposed of. At every archaeological dig large numbers of animal bones are excavated. These provide evidence not only of meat consumption, but also of the nature of the rural economy. The ratio of sheep bones to cattle bones can indicate whether a community was primarily pastoral or agricultural, since cattle were primarily kept for traction rather than milk production. Unfortunately, the sheer quantity of animal bones seems to have prevented anything more than ad hoc attempts at synthesis of the accumulated data. Additionally, on the key dietary question of how much meat was consumed, archaeology can provide no answer. Paleobotanical remains, such as seeds or wood, indicate plant cultivation. However, while faunal remains are found at every archaeological site in large number, floral remains are rare. Interesting results from the studies of plant remains are frequently the result of chance findings due to carbonization or desiccation. Human skeletal remains can also provide relevant information, since bones and teeth can exhibit signs of nutritional stress. For ancient Israel, however, scientific study of human bones encounters both the religio-political issue of disturbing Jewish dead and a paucity of finds.

The discoveries of archaeologists need no less critical interpretation than the biblical texts. A few detailed examples are sufficient to illustrate specific issues related to the Israelite diet. The existence of animal bones need not imply consumption, though it is possible to look for evidence of cut marks, which can indicate that the meat was eaten. Some remains are difficult to detect; fish bones were missed in most early excavations. Cereal and fruit seeds, and wood from fruit trees, have been found frequently at archaeological sites, but vegetables are unlikely to survive. Thus, absence from the archaeological record does not imply absence from the Israelite diet.

Our third set of sources is comparative evidence of diet in other related cultures from the ancient Near East. A great deal of epigraphic and archaeological information is available about many of Israel's ancient Near Eastern neighbors, especially the Egyptian empire and the various empires that dominated Mesopotamia. Yet, as some of the biblical writers were aware, Israel occupied a distinct agricultural niche: "for the land that you are about to enter to occupy is not like the land of Egypt, from which you have come, where you sow your seed and irrigate by foot like a vegetable garden, but the land that you are crossing over to occupy is a land of hills and valleys, watered by rain from the sky" (Deut. 11:10-11). Israelite agriculture was based on capturing rainfall through hillside terraces, while the great empires of Egypt and Mesopotamia relied on river-based irrigation. Climate and environment affected diet too. Barley, rather than wheat, was more common in Egypt and Mesopotamia, and also beer rather than wine. Sharing similar geographical and climatic constraints were Israel's immediate neighbors, such as the Syrian kingdoms and city-states such as Ugarit.

Chronologically proximate are the earlier Bronze Age and the later Hellenistic, Roman, and Byzantine periods. Recent scholarship has shown that the boundaries between these historical periods should not be overemphasized, and that in each case there was significant material and cultural continuity. This is especially the case with food, for while new food-stuffs were introduced at various points in the history of Palestine, the dietary mainstays remained fairly constant in premodern times. Of course, those who study diet in these proximate areas and periods encounter problems in the utilization of written and archaeological sources similar to the ones we have observed for Israel. There is also the problem of the applicability of results from one period or area to that of Israel in the Iron Age. Nevertheless, for many of these locations and periods the scholar has far more data to work with than is the case for ancient Israel.

Fourth, comparative evidence of a quite different sort is provided by modern anthropological research into nonindustrialized societies. Anthropological research on modern communities in Palestine is useful for observing responsiveness to similar ecological constraints. Nevertheless, it should be remembered that the relationship between man and his environment does not flow in only one direction. The environment of ancient Israel had long been managed (or mismanaged) by the time of the Israelite settlement, and has continued to change under human use to the present. Moving further afield, other nonindustrial societies potentially provide evidence of societal structure, patterns of exchange, food distribution, and the use and generation of surpluses. Or, to select another example, the diet and nutrition of contemporary pastoralists can provide a useful comparison to some sections of Israelite society.

Any comparison needs to be considered with constant critical distance. There is the ever present danger that parallels from comparative anthropology will not only inform our understanding of ancient Israelite society but also inadvertently conform it to the parallel society. Scholarship at the end of the nineteenth century, for example, was influenced by encounters with contemporary Bedouin in Palestine. Diet, especially the level of meat consumption, was perceived to be poor among the Palestinian Bedouin, and it was concluded that this was also the case for the ancient Israelites. On the other hand, some recent assessments of the Israelite diet appear to me to be more influenced by the success of Jewish agricultural communities in the twentieth century.[3]

Finally, each of these sources of historical information must be brought into dialogue with scientific knowledge on food production and consumption. This is apparent in Borowski's work on Israelite agriculture, where he utilizes archaeobotanical work on plant domestication. A number of different areas of scientific investigation are relevant to our investigation. First, food production is made possible and constrained by the environment of Israel. The various branches of geography — meteorology, geology, soil science — contribute to our understanding of agricultural possibility in ancient Palestine. Second, nutritional science aids in considering the effect of individual food items in the diet and the overall healthiness of a diet.

Our various sources for reconstructing the Israelite diet provide a number of diverse vistas into the dietary habits of the ancient Israelites. In every instance the evidence for the Israelite diet is fragmentary, and it will be necessary to acknowledge a great deal of uncertainty around it. We might compare the problem to a particularly complex Sudoku puzzle for which we do not have enough numbers to solve every aspect of it, though we will be able to see various parts of the puzzle at the end of our investigation. Remaining with the analogy, it is necessary to utilize all the different sources available to us. Reliance on one sort of data — like pursuing a single strategy in tackling a Sudoku puzzle — will leave us with a very incomplete picture.

In what follows we will first consider the various foodstuffs of the Israelites (section II). This account will depend primarily on the Old Testament text and archaeological finds from Iron Age Israel. Although we will list the various food items, we will attempt to give a critical account of the relative contribution of each to the diet of the Israelites. Second, we will tackle the problem of how healthy the Israelite diet was (section III). In a brief conclusion we will summarize what can be known about the ancient Israelite diet. We will also consider the modern interest in "biblical diets" in the light of our investigations into the ancient Israelite diet (section IV).

SECTION II

WHAT DID THE ISRAELITES EAT?

In this section we examine the different foods that could have contributed
to the diet of the ancient Israelites. We begin with the so-called Mediterranean triad of bread, wine, and olive oil. These were the principal crops of
ancient Palestine and the most significant contributors to the ancient Israelite diet (chapter 3). We then turn to the remaining plant foods — vegetables, pulses, and fruit (chapter 4). Animal products also contributed to the
diet of the Israelites, not only meat and milk, but also fish (chapter 5).
Finally, we turn to the other foods that the Israelites may have consumed
(chapter 6).

CHAPTER 3

The Mediterranean Triad:
Bread, Wine, and Oil

In Israel and many other countries around the Mediterranean, the mainstays of the diet are the so-called Mediterranean triad of bread, wine, and oil. The triad is mentioned in numerous places in the Old Testament. For example, in Hosea 2:8 YHWH identifies "the grain, the wine, and the oil" as the gifts he lavished on Israel. The importance of the triad is also found outside the biblical texts. The Arad inscriptions, for example, make frequent mention of grain, wine, and oil.[1] These crops probably accounted for the vast majority of Israelite land under cultivation. The fertile valleys were planted with cereals, and the hillsides with vineyards and olive orchards.

Wheat and Barley

The staple food for ancient Israel was bread, as indeed it was for her ancient Near Eastern neighbors and the rest of the Mediterranean world. For the typical Israelite, bread or other grain-based foods such as porridge probably provided over half their caloric intake, with estimates varying between 53 and 75 percent.[2] They consumed far more grain than today's Europeans or North Americans. The relationship between bread and nutrition was so close that the Hebrew word *lechem* could cover both "bread" and food in general. In Israel there were two main cereal crops, wheat *(chittim)* and barley *(se'orah)*.[3] The importance of cereal crops is apparent in the Israelite annual festivals, for the completion of the wheat harvest was celebrated at the festival of weeks (Deut. 16:1-12).[4]

The main form of wheat cultivated in ancient Israel was hard or durum wheat (*Triticum durum* [Desf.]).[5] This is a free-threshing variety, in which the grains do not need to be freed from hulls by pounding. This form of wheat is ideally suited to the warm and dry climate of Palestine. It flourishes in regions where annual rainfall is between 500 and 700 millimeters, but can be cultivated when rainfall is above 225 millimeters.[6] In ancient Israel it was sown in November and December and harvested in May.[7] The timely appearance of rain at the beginning of the winter and the continuation of the rainy season until April were necessary to ensure the highest yields. In the Old Testament these two ends of the rainy season are known as the "early rain" and the "later rain" and are viewed as the gift of God (Deut. 11:14).[8] As Borowski observes, "the amount and distribution of rainfall together with soil conditions limit the area of Eretz-Israel where wheat is cultivated to the coastal valleys, the Valley of Jezreel, the Upper Jordan Valley, and the Beth-shan Valley."[9] In addition to the free-threshing wheat, a hulled wheat was also known in Israel. This was probably emmer wheat (*Triticum dicoccum* Schübl), which was known in the Old Testament as *kussemet*. Evidence from across the ancient world suggests that hulled cereals were steadily replaced by free-threshing varieties, although the hulled varieties continued to persist with a minority status. Emmer remained the principal wheat in Egypt even into the Hellenistic period, but in Iron Age Israel the free-threshing durum wheat had already achieved dominance.[10]

The other main cereal crop, barley *(Hordeum vulgare)*, is able to tolerate a far less hospitable environment than wheat. It matures early and its shorter growing season allows it to flourish in areas with low rainfall. Consequently in Israel it could be grown in areas at the limits of agricultural cultivation, such as the northern Negev and the marginal areas of Transjordan.[11] It is also less sensitive than wheat to salinity and alkalinity.[12] This tolerance to alkalinity allows barley to flourish in the chalk and limestone-derived soils that characterize the hill country of Palestine where Israelite settlements were centered.

In many parts of the ancient world barley has been regarded as inferior to wheat.[13] It has a lower extraction rate than wheat and does not rise as well.[14] The assessment of barley in Israel appears to have been no different. Grain offerings were to be made from fine wheat flour *(solet)*,[15] and as offerings to the deity it is appropriate that they are the finest cereal available. The only exception is the offering for the woman suspected of unfaithfulness in Numbers 5, and the negative context of this offering might explain its atypicality.[16] An interesting insight into their relative value is found in 2 Kings. When the siege of Samaria was lifted, "a measure of fine wheat flour was sold for a shekel, and two measures of barley flour for a shekel" (2 Kings 7:16).[17] This judgment is also reflected later in the Mishnah where the exchange rate between wheat and barley is 1:2.[18] The lower status of barley is also seen in the account of Solomon's reign where barley was used alongside straw as horse fodder (1 Kings 4:28).[19] Finally, we should note that in the Roman period Josephus reports that the rich ate wheat bread while the poor ate barley bread.[20]

Wheat and barley could be consumed in a variety of forms.[21] By far the simplest way was to eat the fresh ears (2 Kings 4:42) or to roast the fresh grain in the fire (Josh. 5:11). If threshed, winnowed, and milled, the flour could be used to bake bread. Processing grains for bread was a time-consuming chore performed by women and servants (Jer. 7:18). It has been calculated that three hours' labor with a hand mill per day was needed to produce sufficient flour for a family of five or six.[22] The quality of the flour was determined by how much it was sifted. Ancient technology could achieve only a high extraction (low sieving) rate, and it was not unusual for the flour to be mixed with impurities, such as stone from the milling process. Bread could be baked in a variety of ways. An unleavened cake (*'ugah*) or chapati was probably common. It required only some flour, water, and a little salt, and could be cooked on a hot flat stone that had been heated in the ashes (1 Kings 19:6). A metal griddle over a fire could be used to similar effect (Ezek. 4:3). Ovens *(tannur)* were also known in ancient Israel. In his book on ancient food technology, Curtis describes a *tannur* oven: "Constructed of a clay and gypsum mixture the tannur oven was an upright, beehive-shaped structure. . . . A large opening at the top allowed access to the inside of the oven where the cook would stick moist dough, shaped into circular pancakes, to the walls. She would then seal the opening with clay. The fire, fed with grass and reeds through a smaller opening near the bottom, baked the bread."[23] Grains could also be mixed with water to produce a thin gruel or porridge. In Egypt and Mesopotamia barley was used not only in the production of bread, but also for brewing beer. In these two great river valley civilizations beer was the main alcoholic beverage. In Israel beer consumption was probably rare because of the widespread cultivation of vines on the Palestinian hillsides.[24]

Wine

The ubiquity of the vine and its products in the Old Testament gives suffi-
cient testimony to the economic and social importance of wine in ancient
Israel. In Numbers 13 the prodigious cluster of grapes that the two spies
carry between them is symbolic of the prosperity of the Promised Land.
Time and again in the prophets the vine, or its fruit, is used as a symbol of
Israel.

Vines require an annual rainfall of between 400 and 800 millimeters,
with most of the rain in winter and early spring. Temperatures need to be
above 20°C during fruiting and below 10°C for some of the winter.[25] Vines
thrive best on loamy or stony soil that is not overly fertile. Most of Palestine is ideally suited for viticulture, and the vine had long been cultivated
when the Israelite tribes first settled the land.[26] Establishing a vineyard was
a significant undertaking, and we are fortunate to possess a detailed account in Isaiah 5:1-7.[27] The prophet describes the planting of vines and the
building of a wall, tower, and winepress. Vines were cultivated in a number
of ways, and we know that both allowing the vine to trail along the ground
and training it upward were used in Israel (Ezek. 17:6-8). It is likely that
trailing vines were most common.[28] After four or five years the vine would
begin to produce a usable crop of fruit.

The grape harvest occurred around July and August. At that time the
grape clusters were cut down and placed into baskets. With very little delay
they were taken to nearby winepresses. Many presses carved out of rock
have been discovered in Palestine. They are to be found out in the fields
close to where the grapes were grown. At the presses the grapes were trodden underfoot, with the juice flowing through a conduit into a vat below.
Mechanical means of pressing were probably not introduced until the Hellenistic or Roman period. A number of biblical texts refer to the joyful
shouting and singing that accompanied the treading of the grapes (e.g.,
Isa. 16:10; Jer. 48:33). The process of fermentation probably began in the
collecting vats, and this first stage of fermentation probably took two to
five days. After this the wine was purified, bottled, and placed in storage
chambers for the second, slower stage of fermentation and maturing. This
process lasted six months, during which time carbon dioxide was released
through holes in the jars.[29]

The frequent references to wine in the Old Testament suggest that it
was not only the principal alcoholic beverage, but the principal drink, pe-

riod. Whether it was usually watered down before consumption, as was the practice of the Greeks and Romans,[30] or drunk undiluted is uncertain. Isaiah's disparaging comparison of Judah's righteousness to "wine mixed with water" (1:22) might suggest that there was a preference for undiluted wine. Estimates of the level of wine consumption in ancient Israel have been made on the basis of the remains of wine production facilities and storage rooms. Shimon Dar estimates up to a liter of wine per person per day.[31] Even if wine was spoiled, it could still be used, as is evident from its use as an adjunct to bread in Ruth 2:14.

The climatic demands of the vine ensured that viticulture had a very small role in Egypt and Mesopotamia. Here beer was the principal beverage, and wine was restricted to the elites. Some scholars have equated the biblical *shekar*, which appears on a number of occasions in the Old Testament, with beer. It is perhaps more likely that this was a generic term for alcoholic drinks.[32] The esteem of wine in Egypt and Mesopotamia led to wine being a profitable export for the Israelite states.[33] At Ashkelon and Gibeon archaeological finds have demonstrated the existence of industrial-scale wine production in the eighth and seventh centuries B.C.[34] These were developed to supply the neo-Assyrian empire. In a later period it is striking that the biblical historians draw attention to vinedressers being exempted from the exile by Nebuchadnezzar (2 Kings 25:12). It is likely, then, that Palestine was valued during the periods of Assyrian and Babylonian hegemony principally for its ability to supply wine for consumption in the royal court and by elites.

Olive Oil

The olive is the third member of the so-called Mediterranean triad. Its importance to the ancient Israelite economy is apparent in Jotham's parable, where it is the first to be offered the kingship of the trees. Its response is, "Shall I stop producing my rich oil by which gods and mortals are honored?" (Judg. 9:9). The celebrated oil could be used in a variety of ways — for food, cooking, lighting, cultic offerings, ointment, and anointing for office.[35] The consumption of the fruit was probably unknown to the ancient Israelites. The fruit is bitter and needs to be pickled or salted to be eaten. These processing techniques were not introduced into Palestine until the Hellenistic or Roman period.[36]

The olive tree is best adapted to the Mediterranean climate and thrives on well-drained sandy or rocky soils.[37] It requires an average rainfall of at least 400 millimeters, warm summers, and cool winters.[38] In Palestine the olive would have been particularly suited to the rocky slopes of the Israelite highlands. In October the fruit was harvested by beating the branches with a stick (Deut. 24:20).[39] The olives were gathered in baskets to be taken to a production facility where oil was extracted through a three-stage process: crushing the olives, pressing the mash, and separating the oil from the watery lees. The fruit could be pressed in a variety of ways. It could be trodden underfoot in rock-cut basins,[40] pounded in a mortar, or, on a larger scale, crushed with a stone on a flat slab.[41] In Iron Age II large-scale processing became a possibility with the proliferation of the beam press.[42] A lever-and-weight mechanism was used to crush olives under the wooden beam, with the oil collecting in a basin below.[43] The increased capacity of oil production facilities, such as at seventh century B.C. Ekron, is part of the evidence for the export of olive oil from Palestine to other parts of the ancient Near East, especially Mesopotamia. With oil having such an important role in the economy of the region, it is not surprising that many olive groves were subjected to royal control (1 Sam. 8:14; 1 Chron. 27:28).

Olive oil was probably an important component of the Israelite diet. In the later Roman period, the Mishnah prescribed that an estranged wife be provided with a food basket that included oil as one of the four foodstuffs. The husband was to provide 160-230 grams per week, an amount of oil that would have contributed 11 percent of the overall calories.[44] Some scholars suggest that oil consumption could have been even higher, around 330-380 grams per week.[45] It is surprising, however, that the Old Testament says so little about oil as a foodstuff. In the account of Elijah and the widow of Zarephath, the oil is mixed with flour to make a cake (1 Kings 17:12-13). Other biblical passages suggest that it was a valuable product associated with good eating (Ezek. 16:13, 19; Isa. 25:6). On the basis of this biblical evidence and the Samaria and Arad ostraca, Frankel suggests that "in Iron Age Judaea and Israel . . . olive oil was a staple product of importance, although probably not available to the poorest part of the population."[46] This may be overstated, but certainly we must reckon with the possibility that the level of olive oil consumption varied markedly with social class, and may have become more available during Iron Age II.

CHAPTER 4

Vegetables, Pulses, and Fruit

Various other plant foods were grown and consumed in Israel besides the Mediterranean triad. These include vegetables, pulses, and, of course, fruit. Unfortunately, for a number of reasons it is difficult to assess exactly what contribution they made to the Israelite diet. First, the soft flesh of vegetation and fruit rots easily and rarely leaves any trace in the archaeological record unless carbonized or desiccated. Second, these foods are either eaten raw or prepared by boiling, and consequently no technical implements are needed that might be discovered in excavations. Third, the ancient Israelites seem to have placed particular values on vegetation and fruit that affect their appearance in the biblical texts. They had a low view of vegetables, but fruit was esteemed highly. These factors need to be kept in mind as we examine these components of the Israelite diet.

Vegetables

Vegetables were poorly regarded in ancient Israel, and this negative view is occasionally traded on in the Old Testament. In the book of Proverbs the sages remind the young student who may be entranced by a rich meal that "a meal of vegetables where there is friendship is better than a fatted ox and hatred" (Prov. 15:17).[1] In other words, in the Israelite hierarchy of foods, meat is at the top and vegetables are near the bottom. Another well-known example is the story of Daniel and his companions who forgo the rich Babylonian fare for a vegetable diet (Dan. 1). Their healthy appearance after ten days is counterintuitive and regarded as miraculous. According to the creation story in Genesis 1, cereals and fruits are given to humanity for food, while vegetation is given to the animals. There is only one enumeration of vegetables in the Old Testament, in Numbers 11:5: "the cucumbers, melons, leeks, onions and garlic." The context is noteworthy, for these foods are associated with Egypt and the Israelites' sinful craving for food in the wilderness.

The low assessment of vegetables cannot be disassociated from the material realities of Israelite agriculture. Vegetable cultivation was more developed in Egypt and Mesopotamia where the irrigation that a vegetable garden requires was more commonly practiced (cf. Deut. 11:10-11). Nevertheless, the occasional mention of vegetables does suggest that they played some role in the Israelite diet.[2] However, those who ate vegetables may have been at the extremes of Israelite society: the wealthy few who could afford to set aside land for a vegetable garden (cf. 1 Kings 21), and the poor who may have used wild vegetation and other foods to supplement their diet: leafy plants, bulbs, wild fruits and nuts, roots, mushrooms.[3] In the Iron Age significant parts of Palestine were still covered by thick forests, especially in the north. These forests would have provided ideal environments in which to forage for wild vegetation. Wild plants may also have been utilized by a larger part of the population during famine conditions. An interesting account in 2 Kings 4 narrates the consumption of wild plants for a stew during a period of famine. The dangers are also described, for a poisonous plant is gathered that requires the intervention of the prophet to neutralize.

Pulses

It is difficult to ascertain exactly how important pulses — that is, annual leguminous crops — were in the diets of the ancient Israelites. They have made only a shallow impression in the Old Testament text, with the lentil referred to four times and the broad bean twice. The lentil (*'adashim*) is native to Palestine and is a winter grown crop. It produces pods that contain small flat circular seeds (3-6 millimeters in diameter).[4] The play on the red color of Jacob's broth in Genesis 25 suggests that red lentils were known in Israel. The broad bean (*pol*), sometimes known as the horse bean or the fava bean, has oblong seeds (6-13 millimeters in diameter) in a large, thick pod. It prefers well-drained clay soils and a mild climate.[5] Other pulses are known from their appearance in Iron Age strata from archaeological excavations: field peas, chickpeas, bitter vetch, and fenugreek. Field peas are a winter crop that does best on "medium or slightly impoverished soils such as well drained clay loams of limestone origins,"[6] that is, the type of soil characteristic of the Israelite highlands. In the ancient world they were cultivated for the mature dry seed, not the immature "green" seed familiar in Europe and North America.[7] Chickpeas require warm, semiarid conditions and would have been grown in the dry season, planted in the spring after the winter rains.[8] Bitter vetch has small pods that contain three or four angular seeds (3-4 millimeters in diameter). As the name suggests, the seeds are toxic to humans, but the toxicity can be removed by soaking in water. Since at least Roman times it has been used mainly as fodder, "for it is regarded as very inferior for human consumption and is only eaten by the very poor, or in times of famine."[9] This may already have been the case in the Iron Age. Fenugreek has seeds that are highly aromatic and is used in India as a condiment.[10] Other leguminous plants, such as common vetch and grass pea, are known from Early Bronze Age archaeological finds and may also have been cultivated in Iron Age Palestine.[11]

An argument could certainly be made that pulses played a more substantial role in Israelite diets than the Old Testament or archaeology might lead us to suspect.[12] First, the dominance of the Mediterranean triad in the consciousness of the ancient Israelite writers may well have resulted in other relatively important foodstuffs being almost ignored in the biblical texts. In addition, pulses probably endured the same low level of esteem that vegetables sustained. Consequently, it might not be amiss to reckon that pulses had an important role to play, as indeed they probably did in later periods. It has been argued that they played a significant role in Palestinian diets during the Roman period.[13] They are mentioned relatively frequently in the Talmud,[14] and they were also a significant component of the "food basket" that the Mishnaic sages required former husbands to give their estranged wives (see chapter 7). Magen Broshi calculates that pulses supplied approximately 17 percent of the caloric intake in the wife's "food basket."[15]

Diets with a significant component of pulses would have had certain nutritional benefits. For the majority of Israelites, for whom meat was a rarity, pulses would have been the principal source of protein. "In traditional agricultural communities pulses served — and still serve — as a main meat substitute."[16] They could also have played an important role agriculturally alongside cereal crops. Wheat and barley quickly exhaust the soil's fertility and supply of nitrogen. Leguminous crops utilize nitrogen from the air and ultimately return it to the soil. This form of crop rotation was certainly employed extensively in the Roman Empire.[17] The question is whether the same is true earlier in Iron Age Palestine.[18] The Old Testament suggests only the practice of fields kept fully fallow, rather than a system involving the rotation of crops. However, the system of leaving all fields fallow during the sabbatical year seems impractical agriculturally and an example of a priestly ideal.[19] Consequently, passages like Leviticus 25 can provide only limited guidance to the fallowing systems employed in ancient Israel. David Hopkins is right to argue that we should keep open the possibility of legume rotation, "though the probability that legumes played a significant role in early Iron Age agriculture is low."[20] The high precipitation requirement of some pulses, over 400 millimeters, would have restricted their use to only some parts of Palestine and made them vulnerable during dry years.[21] It might be that pulses were grown as garden plants, on a small scale with irrigation, rather than as field crops in rotation with cereals.

Along with the dietary and agricultural benefits, pulses also have the advantage that after the seeds have been dried they can be kept for long periods. They can also be used in a variety of ways. Roasting the seeds was practiced in antiquity, and this may explain 2 Samuel 17:28 where lentils and broad beans are mentioned alongside roasted grain. The seeds could be prepared in a broth, as Jacob did in Genesis 25. Finally, Ezekiel is reported to have combined lentils and broad beans with cereals to make a bread cake (Ezek. 4:9), though this may reflect famine conditions induced by siege rather than usual culinary practice.[22]

Fruit

Fruit trees played an important role in the economy of ancient Israel and in the Israelite diet. This was principally through the vine, the olive, and the fig. Other fruits were cultivated in Israel — the sycamore fig, the date palm, and the pomegranate — but their contribution was relatively insignificant.[23] This is easily obscured because fruit had emotional and symbolic resonances in the Old Testament that tend to exaggerate its importance. In particular, fruit trees represent the divine gift of food requiring no human labor. Humanity's primeval origins were, according to Genesis 2, in a garden filled with numerous fruit trees. Palestine too is gifted to the Israelites, and when the spies return to the people in the wilderness they come bearing grapes, pomegranates, and figs (Num. 13:23). It is not surprising, then, that when the bounty of the land is described in Deuteronomy 8, the Mediterranean triad is interwoven with fruits and fruit products: "a land of wheat and barley, of vines and fig trees and pomegranates, a land of olive trees and fruit syrup, a land where you may eat bread without scarcity, where you will lack nothing" (vv. 8-9).[24] Thus the frequent appearance of fruit in the biblical texts may give a misleading impression of its significance in the Israelite diet.

We have already observed that a significant proportion of the Israelite hill country would have been given over to the cultivation of vines and olive trees. Although grapes were principally used for making wine, they could also be consumed fresh during harvesting (Deut. 23:24; Num. 6:3). Dried raisins could be preserved for later usage *(tsimmuqim)*, including being mashed into a cake *('ashishah)*.

The fig (*Ficus carica* L.), Hebrew *te'enah*, is mentioned frequently in the Old Testament. It is native to Palestine and thrives best on well-drained hillslopes with a thin soil;[25] it needs as little as 300 millimeters of rain. It has two crops, the first in June and the second in August or September. The importance of the fig is apparent in Jotham's parable; the fig is one of the candidates, together with the olive and the vine, for the leadership of the trees (Judg. 9:8-15). The destruction of the fig tree is a frequent motif in the prophetic condemnation of Israel's breaking of the covenant (e.g., Joel 1:7). The fig was also used as a metaphor for the nation and her people, most famously in Jeremiah's parable of the good and bad figs (Jer. 24). In the national ideal everyone would have his own vine and fig tree (Mic. 4:4). The fig can be eaten fresh or dried. Dried figs could be stored individually or mashed into a cake *(debelah)*. According to Borowski, "the importance of the fig tree as one of the mainstays of biblical economy cannot be overemphasized."[26] This statement can be supported by observing how frequently figs are mentioned in the Old Testament, particularly alongside other staples in food assemblages (e.g., 1 Sam. 25:18; 30:12; 2 Sam. 16:1-2; Jer. 40:10, 12; 1 Chron. 12:40). Support from a later period is found in the Mishnaic "food basket" of the estranged wife where figs are the fourth component of the ration contributing 16 percent of the overall caloric intake.[27]

The sycamore fig (*Ficus sycomorus* L.), Hebrew *shiqmim*, was very common in some of the warmer parts of Israel, giving rise to the proverbial expression "as numerous as the sycamores of the Shephelah" (e.g., 1 Kings 10:27). According to 1 Chronicles 27:28, these belonged to the royal estate. If so, they were probably cultivated primarily for their wood rather than their fruit; though not as valuable as Lebanon's famous cedars, the long straight beams were useful in construction. If this was the case, it is important to observe that the "treatment that promotes the growth of straight, smooth limbs inhibits the growth of fruit."[28] Those trees that were kept for their fruit would have produced a steady supply of figs that are smaller and inferior to those produced by the common fig.[29]

The date palm, Hebrew *tamar*, requires a hot and dry climate. Consequently cultivation in Israel was restricted to the coast and the Jordan Valley.[30] Dates can be eaten both fresh and dried; they can also be boiled down to a syrup, so-called date honey. Interestingly, although the Old Testament refers to the date a number of times, only one reference concerns the fruit (Joel 1:12).

The pomegranate, Hebrew *rimmon*, is listed as one of the seven agricultural products of the land of Israel in Deuteronomy 8:8. A deciduous bush or small tree, it produces large fruit containing small juicy seeds. Its seeds can be eaten fresh or its juice fermented for wine. The pomegranate probably played a relatively minor role in the diet of the Israelites, but it possessed a number of symbolic resonances that are utilized by the biblical writers.[31] It is a symbol of both human fertility, as occurs in the Song of Songs, and the fruitfulness of the land (e.g., Num. 13:23). The numerous seeds in each fruit probably suggested this association with fertility. Artistic representations of the pomegranate also adorned the fringes of the priestly robe (Exod. 28:33) and the capitals of the temple pillars (1 Kings 7:20).

A number of words referring to fruit in the Old Testament have resisted confident identification. *Tappuach* has traditionally been translated "apple," but identifications with quince and apricot have also been offered.[32] None of these three trees is native to the Near East. Though many insist that *tappuach* is not an "apple," Zohary and Hopf argue that the quince and apricot do not appear in the Near East until classical times, while the apple existed on the periphery of the ancient Near East for a long period.[33] The discovery of apple remains at Kadesh Barnea may also lend support to the traditional identification.[34] The meaning of *baka'* (2 Sam. 5:23-24; Ps. 84:6; 1 Chron. 14:14-15) is even more difficult to ascertain.

A variety of edible nuts were known in ancient Israel, although their dietary role was almost certainly minor. The almond, Hebrew *shaqed*, appears occasionally in the Old Testament, principally because of the beauty of its blossom (e.g., Exod. 25:33-34; 37:19-20). The pistachio, Hebrew *botnim*, is also mentioned in the Old Testament. It should be observed that both almond and pistachio were among the *delicacies* of Palestine that Jacob sent to Egypt (Gen. 43:11). We should therefore probably assume that they appeared only in the diets of wealthy elites.

CHAPTER 5

Meat, Milk, Birds, and Fish

Meat

For the inhabitants of Palestine throughout the historical periods, meat has meant primarily one of the four domesticated animals: sheep, goats, cattle, and pigs. The breeding and marketing of these animals was an important component of the Palestinian economy in earlier periods and also during the time of the Israelite kingdoms. As we have already seen, meat was highly valued, especially in comparison with vegetables. Animal flesh was also the archetypal offering for God, especially the fatty portions. For some periods of Israel's history, meat could be consumed only if it had been offered at the sanctuary. Although the interpretation of Cain and Abel's sacrifices has long been a subject of controversy, it is perhaps not insignificant that Cain's grain offering is valued less highly than Abel's animal offering. The divine preference in this story matched the general preference of the Israelites.

Although the Passover lamb was to be roasted over a flame, this was probably unusual (Exod. 12:9). It appears that the ordinary practice in ancient Israel was to cook meat by boiling it in a pot to create a broth or stew (e.g., 1 Sam. 2:13; Ezek. 24:3-5). This also appears to have been the practice in Mesopotamia. From Babylonia we have three cuneiform tablets that date from the Old Babylonian period (ca. 1700 B.C.) that describe briefly the preparation of various meat and vegetable dishes. The meat was boiled in water together with alliaceous vegetables — onions, garlic, leeks — and herbs and spices — cumin, coriander.[1] Although these were probably elite meals, the detailed recipes are an unparalleled discovery and may provide an indication of how meat was prepared in ancient Israel.

In the period after the exile an attempt was made to regulate the consumption of meat through the dietary laws that are found in Leviticus 11 and Deuteronomy 14. These provide a detailed list of which mammals, birds, fish, and reptiles may be eaten and which are prohibited. The dietary laws in their present literary form date from late in Israel's history. To what extent the forbidden animals were considered taboo in an earlier period is a matter of intense discussion. Some of the lists, for example, the twenty forbidden species of birds, probably reflect an exercise in priestly categorization, rather than foods that were readily available and considered for eating. Some forbidden animals, however, may reflect traditional taboos from the early Iron Age, and the pig is one of the most likely candidates. Consequently it is necessary to draw on evidence other than the dietary laws in Leviticus and Deuteronomy when considering meat consumption in Israel.

Fortunately not only does the Bible frequently touch upon the production and consumption of meat, but significant evidence of it can be found in the archaeological record as well. Animal bones are one of the most frequent finds during an archaeological excavation.[2] In earlier excavations they were usually discarded as archaeologists had little use for them, but in the last thirty years examination of animal bones has become a sophisticated science revealing significant information about the ways the ancient Israelites and their neighbors utilized domesticated animals. We will consider this evidence in more detail in chapter 10, and it will allow us to build a nuanced picture of the changing patterns of meat consumption in ancient Israel. For the moment it is just necessary to give a brief account of the animals that were consumed.

Alongside sheep, goats, cattle, and pigs, the Israelites also kept other domestic animals, such as camels, donkeys, and dogs. These had other roles within the local economy and were not generally utilized for food. Thus, the discovery of bones from these animals at archaeological sites is not usually a sign of consumption. In rare cases, however, bones have been discovered with cut marks indicating that meat was cut off with a knife, presumably for consumption. So, for example, there are cut marks on dogs and donkeys at Late Bronze Age Lachish, and on camels and donkeys at Iron Age Hesban.[3] Both cities were non-Israelite settlements, but there is also the story of the siege of Samaria when, it is said, "an ass's head was sold for four pieces of silver" (2 Kings 6:25), an unappetizing meal that is probably meant to illustrate the desperate measures to which the besieged Israelites were reduced. We may therefore assume that consumption of other domesticated animals was rare. From the perspective of the biblical food laws, of course, all these animals were unclean.

In Deuteronomy 12 the Israelites are permitted to slaughter domestic animals at home rather than at the sanctuary. This appears to be an innovative practice, and the writer appeals to the way the gazelle and deer were killed and eaten. Since they are not sacrificial animals, they could be killed outside the sanctuary and eaten. In this law the gazelle and the deer function as the archetypal wild mammals that the Israelites might consume. This account fits the archaeological picture well. Wild animals were rarely consumed in Iron Age Palestine, but the majority that were eaten belonged to these two species. The deer is generally found more frequently in archaeological finds than the gazelle. Deer could belong to one of three species: the red deer *(Cervus elaphus)*, the fallow deer *(Dama mesopotamica)*, or the roe deer *(Capreolus capreolus)*. The first two species, in particular, cannot always be distinguished easily in archaeological excavations, and most cases are reported in excavation reports as fallow deer. The mountain gazelle *(Gazella gazella)* is native to the mountains of Palestine.

The archaeological evidence shows that wild animals made only a slight contribution to the Israelite diet. In the pre-Israelite period more wild animals were consumed, and the decline from earlier periods is part of a wider pattern of human exploitation of the Palestinian environment that led to a loss of habitat for wild animals.[4] Against the background of this trajectory the Late Bronze Age and the early Iron Age show slightly higher levels of wild animal consumption. This probably reflects the economic stress and impoverishment of these periods with parts of the population resorting to foraging and hunting for some of their sustenance.[5] In addition, there were still significant areas of uncultivated land particularly in the north of Palestine, and higher levels of wild animal remains can be observed in northern sites.[6] Hunting, then, appears to have been a fairly minor part of the Iron Age economy of Palestine. In some areas in the north it may have had a more important role where hunting for gazelle and deer took place. Other animals, such as bear, wild boar, lion, and hippopotamus, have occasionally been found in the archaeological record. These were probably opportunistic kills.[7]

Milk and Dairy Products

The domesticated animals were important not only for providing a supply of meat, but also for the secondary products they provided. Goats and, to a lesser extent, sheep were particularly valuable because they produced milk for part of the year. In ancient Palestine milk and dairy products were an important food source.[8] This was especially true for pastoralists, but also for others in ancient Israel. In the Near East the animal primarily associated with milk production has been the goat. Cattle were utilized primarily for traction, and sheep provided wool. This association is clear in the rabbinic period; Rabbi Nachman is reported to have said, "a goat for its milk, a ewe for its fleece . . . oxen for ploughing."[9] The association of milk with goats can already be found in the Old Testament: a kid must not be cooked in its mother's milk (Deut. 14:21), and according to Proverbs 27:26-27, "lambs will provide your clothing, and male goats the price of a field; there will be enough goats' milk for your food."[10] The reason for preferring goats to sheep is clear enough. Sheep have about half the annual milk yield of goats, and lactate for about three months, while goats can be milked for up to five months.[11]

Fresh milk, then, was available only in the first half of the year, but it also quickly soured in the heat. Consequently milk was processed into ghee or "cheese," and rarely drunk fresh. It is difficult to judge whether biblical references to *chalab*, the word usually translated "milk," are to be understood as fresh milk or processed dairy products. This latter possibility is supported by a term such as *charitse hechalab* (1 Sam. 17:18). A translation "slices of milk" makes no sense, so in this expression *chalab* is probably to be understood as a form of "cheese." It is certainly misleading, therefore, to suggest, as Borowski does on the basis of Judges 5:25, that "whenever possible, milk was drunk to quench thirst."[12] The processing of milk involves allowing it to sour and then turning it into either ghee or cheese. Ghee, or clarified butter, is formed by churning the milk in a goatskin. This produces lumps of butter and buttermilk. It is then boiled and, when cooled, forms ghee, which can be stored for a long time. "Cheese" is made of fermented sour milk or buttermilk, which is dried in small balls.[13] When the cheese is to be used, it can be restored to a liquid state by adding water.[14] Whichever of these dairy products is to be associated with Hebrew *chem'ah*, it is likely that both were known to the Israelites.[15]

Many of the biblical texts associate dairy products with luxury and

35

abundance. The Promised Land, as we have already discussed, is characterized as flowing with milk and honey. In a number of accounts of hospitality, milk is one of the choice foods presented to the guest (Gen. 18:8; Judg. 4:19; 2 Sam. 17:29).[16] In Job 21:24 the rich die with their loins full of milk.[17] The association of milk with pastoralists in the Old Testament, such as Abraham and Jael, suggests unsurprisingly that as a foodstuff it was consumed in greater quantities by those who owned sheep and goats.

Birds

Biblical and archaeological evidence reveals that various birds were consumed by the Israelites. During all periods of Israel's history the consumption of fowl was probably fairly small. We cannot be too confident in our judgment because bird remains are not often recovered from archaeological sites. Bird bones are fragile, and because it is expensive and time-consuming to sieve the earth removed during an archaeological excavation, they are often a chance discovery. The Israelites consumed both wild and domesticated birds. Among the former we can number quail and partridge, and among the latter, geese, ducks, and pigeons.[18]

Much controversy surrounds the question whether chicken was consumed in ancient Israel. No mention is made of chicken in the Old Testament. However, bones have been recovered from numerous Iron Age sites, and have even been found in Bronze Age strata at Shiloh.[19] Despite this, Hesse and Wapnish express skepticism: "The dating of these associations in our view, however, is dubious, since, in many cases, contamination from later deposits cannot be ruled out. Further, when chicken arrives in a Levantine economy, it tends to be a rather dramatic event, one recorded by dozens or even hundreds of bone finds."[20] The confusing archaeological picture may strengthen the case for an alternative solution. A couple of Iron Age seals picture fighting cocks, and it is possible that chickens were introduced into ancient Israel as fighting animals and only later exploited as a source of meat.[21] Chickens are, of course, a source of eggs, which previously could have been obtained only from the nests of wild birds. Again caution is necessary because, although consumption of eggs seems to us a natural consequence of keeping chickens, this does not seem to have been the case in the ancient world. In an examination of the history of the consumption of chicken eggs, Stadelman warns that "it is doubtful that egg production was, initially at least, a very important reason for maintaining the bird."[22]

At first glance the instructions about the consumption of birds in the biblical dietary laws would appear to offer some help to those interested in reconstructing the Israelite diet. A close examination reveals a number of peculiarities in the list. There is neither a list of permitted birds nor any criteria for distinguishing clean and unclean. Instead, twenty prohibited species are listed (not all of which can be identified with confidence) and described as "detestable" (Lev. 11:13-19). It is usual to suggest that the unclean birds were carrion eaters or raptors; they consumed food elsewhere defined as unclean and were therefore unclean themselves. Whatever the reason, the birds prohibited are very unlikely to have appeared on the Israelite table, for as Origen observed already in the third century A.D., who would contemplate eating some of these birds even if they could catch them?[23]

Fish

One of the most surprising discoveries from recent archaeological excavations in Palestine is the extensive evidence for the consumption of fish. It had been assumed with good reason that the ancient Israelites rarely ate fish. First, the Israelite kingdoms were based in the central highlands of Palestine and only rarely controlled the coast of Palestine. Even when they did, this part of the Mediterranean coastline offers very few natural harbors. Second, Israel boasts very few rivers that are perennial and can support freshwater fish. Finally, it was often observed that fish were absent from the Israelite sacrificial regulations. This was taken to mean that the early Israelites originally occupied an area without access to a regular supply of fish.

The discovery of fish remains from almost every recent excavation requires that these conclusions be abandoned. The fragility of fish bones and the only occasional use of sieving make the number and variety of fish bones discovered throughout Palestine even more surprising. The remains indicate that some of the inhabitants of Palestine had access to a variety of freshwater and saltwater fish. The fresh fish include the Nile catfish, St. Peter's Fish, and mouthbreeders. They most probably originated in the closest major freshwater sources: the Yarkon, the Sea of Galilee, and the Jordan. The discovery of another freshwater fish, the Nile perch (*Lates niloticus*), at sites throughout Palestine is more intriguing. This fish likely originated in the Nile and, after being smoked or dried, was imported to Palestine.[24] The discovery of bones from the Nile perch elsewhere in the eastern Mediterranean suggests that even inland Israelite cities belonged to a wide trade network in which fish were exchanged.[25] Marine fish discovered in archaeological excavations include sea breams, groupers, meagers, and gray mullets. Many of the fish came from the eastern Mediterranean, but in Iron Age II some of them even came from the Red Sea.[26] Before being transported inland they must have been preserved by salting or drying. Biblical evidence for the trade of fish can be found in the book of Nehemiah. In Nehemiah's time the Tyrians traded fish (Neh. 13:16), and one of the city gates was known as the fish gate (12:39). It is likely that the fish market was located here.

In later periods fish became the typical Sabbath dish for observant Jews, but it is unclear to what extent fish played a role in the ancient Israelite diet. During the Iron Age fish appears to have become more readily available.[27] Nevertheless, even in the later years of the Israelite and Judean monarchies the costs of purchasing fish that had been transported over a considerable distance must have been high. As a result, the consumption of fish was probably restricted to the elites in major urban centers and to those who lived in the Jordan Valley or along other major rivers.[28]

CHAPTER 6

Condiments and Other Foods

Various other foods were known to the Israelites. Sesame seeds, for example, have been discovered at Iron Age sites in Palestine. There is no mention of "sesame" in the Bible, and its role in diet must be considered negligible.[1] More significant, at least because of the biblical references to it, was "honey," an item consumed by the Israelites and exported (Ezek. 27:17). Hebrew has a number of words for honey, not only *debash*, the most common, but also *nopet* and *ya'ar. Debash*, which is typically rendered "honey" in English translation, should usually be understood to refer to a sweet syrup produced by boiling down fruit. This can be demonstrated from 2 Chronicles 31:5, where *debash* is listed as one of the products of the field alongside grain, wine, and oil. Further evidence is provided by similar words in two other Semitic languages, Akkadian and Arabic, which also refer to fruit syrups. Since the Israelites had few sweeteners, it is not surprising, however, that the word *debash* could also be used for bee honey.[2]

Direct evidence for beekeeping in ancient Israel is absent from the Bible. Indeed, it is striking that on the two occasions that *debash* clearly refers to bee honey in the Old Testament, wild honey is in view. In Judges 14 Samson observes a bees' nest in the corpse of a lion, and in 1 Samuel 14 Jonathan comes upon a honeycomb while pursuing Philistines. The absence is also confirmed by archaeological excavations, though very recently it has been claimed that beehives were discovered in tenth-century or early-ninth-century strata at Tel Rehov.[3] On the basis of this textual and archaeological silence, both Dalman, and Brothwell and Brothwell, argued that beekeeping was not practiced until the Hellenistic period.[4] Neufeld presents a different view for the wider ancient Near East: "It is inconceivable that within a framework of such highly sophisticated agricultural conditions, where vigorous attacks on hunger brought about ingenious activities, the importance of increasing the productivity of bees through beekeeping was either overlooked or neglected. This would be extraordinary, particularly in an area which is especially well suited to bee-keeping and honey production."[5] Certainly apiculture was virtually absent from Mesopotamia until the first millennium, for according to his own testimony, the eighth-century Assyrian king Shamash-resh-usur introduced the practice. In Egypt, however, it was well developed. It is not unreasonable to imagine that at some point, possibly in the Iron Age, it was introduced into Israel from that source, rather than as an export from Greece during the Hellenistic period.

The Old Testament mentions a number of condiments. By far the most common is salt, which is referred to throughout the Old Testament. It may have been valued for its preservative function, but it was also known to be useful for flavoring food (Job 6:6). Since levels of salt consumption depend upon taste and availability, Broshi argues that "in Palestine, where salt was readily available from the Dead Sea and Mount Sodom and from drying pans, both natural and artificial, along the Mediterranean, we may assume a high salt consumption."[6] This may be truer of later periods than of the early Iron Age when the Israelite tribes were restricted to the highland areas.

Isaiah 28:25, 27 attest to the cultivation of cumin and black cumin in Israel.[7] Coriander was also known (Exod. 16:31; Num. 11:7), though whether this was grown or collected from the wild is uncertain.[8] Only condiments produced or grown locally would have been familiar to the greater part of the population. The Old Testament refers to some imported spices — for example, cinnamon and saffron — but their exorbitant cost would probably have restricted their use to a few elites in the major cities. It is worth noting that spices were included among the exotic gifts that the queen of Sheba is said to have brought Solomon (1 Kings 10:2). Spices were clearly never common in Israel because the narrator informs us that "never again was there as much spice as that which the Queen of Sheba gave to King Solomon" (10:10). The mention of particular spices may be more a case of literary exotica, utilized for rhetorical purposes by the biblical authors, than reportage representative of the typical Israelite diet.

HOW WELL DID THE ISRAELITES EAT?

A number of different foodstuffs were consumed in ancient Israel, but how well did the Israelites eat? As we have seen, we cannot assume that the average Israelite had a balanced or varied diet. Just because a food is mentioned in the biblical text or found in the archaeological record does not mean it was regularly consumed. Exploring the adequacy of the ancient Israelite diet is a difficult problem. The limitations of our knowledge mean that we cannot address the subject in an entirely conclusive manner. Some have attempted to do so by creating theoretical models of the production capacity of Israelite sites. The potential of these models and their difficulties need to be considered (chapter 7). Critically used, these models provide solutions for part of the puzzle, but they need to be augmented with other considerations. The following chapters outline the areas that need to be included. These include a careful analysis of the role that climate and environment had on food production (chapter 8), the possibility that food shortage and famine may have resulted from poor weather or socioeconomic crises (chapter 9), the role played by meat in the Israelite diet (chapters 10 and 11), the problems of food distribution (chapter 12), and the evidence for the existence of significant nutritional deficiencies in the Israelite population (chapter 13).

CHAPTER 7

Modeling the Israelite Diet

In our examination of the foodstuffs that we know were consumed in ancient Israel, we have learned how difficult it is to determine what contribution they made to the diet of the average Israelite. It would be wonderful if we could assume that the appearance of a food in the Bible or archaeological excavations was roughly representative of its role in the Israelite diet. A little reflection reveals that this is not the case. Consequently in our examination of the various foodstuffs that were consumed, we began to reflect critically on the question of how frequently certain foods may have appeared on the Israelite table. Vegetables and pulses, for example, though rarely mentioned in the biblical text and often absent in archaeological finds, may well have been important components of the Israelite diet. If the appearance of foodstuffs in the biblical text cannot be taken as representative, are there other ways we can provide a model of the diet of the average Israelite?

Textual sources for a later period appear at first glance to be more promising, and since the Palestinian diet was probably relatively stable over a long time, it might be possible to extrapolate backward from them. Frequently mentioned in scholarly literature on the Roman and Byzantine period is the food basket that is prescribed for the estranged wife in the Mishnah. We have already mentioned it in previous chapters. The Mishnah requires that husbands who have separated from their wives continue to provide them with food. "He who maintains his wife by a third party may not provide for her less than two *qabs* of wheat or four *qabs* of barley [per week]. Said R. Yose, 'only R. Ishmael ruled that barley may be given to her, for he was near Edom.' And one pays over to her a half-*qab* of pulse, a half-*log* of oil, and a *qab* of dried figs or a *maneh* of fig cake. And if he does not have it, he provides instead food of some other type."[1] There can be no doubt that this information is useful for the historian of Roman Palestine, and with qualification for earlier periods too. In particular, the description provides a clear account of the staple foods and some indication of their proportional contribution to the diet of the period. Cereal is the most important component of the basket in terms of calorie contribution. Pulses and figs were clearly also significant, even if it might be difficult to discern that from the biblical material. We might also observe that wine and meat are absent, as well as fish and dairy products.

Some have wished to go further and argue that the Mishnaic food basket shows that the diet of Palestine was nutritious and satisfying. Magen Broshi, for example, writes:

> According to the United Nations Food and Agriculture Organization (FAO), the recommended daily caloric intake for women during their childbearing years is 2090-2220 calories; for women beyond the childbearing age, it is 1540-1980 calories . . . the rabbis' recommended diet comes close to the FAO's recommended intake. However, because these foods and quantities are not grouped by a professional dietitian, one can only view them as a basic guide. In addition, there is the food for the seventh day, for if the husband had to provide for his wife on weekdays, the same husband had to feed her on the Sabbath, when the menu was richer and more diversified. In addition, the estranged wife might have been able to supplement her diet with food purchased either with the little money that her husband was obliged to give her weekly (a coin called *maah*) or with her own income.[2]

According to Broshi, the food basket was sufficiently nutritious, even without any possible supplementary items. Shimon Dar also draws on the Mishnaic basket and is even more confident: "An analysis of the written sources from the Roman-Byzantine period, in addition to archaeological discoveries, teaches us about the varied and satisfying diet which the inhabitants of Palestine enjoyed in ancient times. It appears that the calorific value did not fall short of that of the present day."[3]

There are a couple of problems with Broshi's and Dar's arguments for the Roman and Byzantine diet. First, the Mishnaic food basket is prescriptive rather than descriptive, and consequently cannot address actual diet in Roman Palestine. To what extent the weekly diet of women matched this prescription we do not know. What we do know is that the rabbinic sages were broadly aware of the amount of food that a mature woman should eat in a week. The limitations of the Mishnaic evidence are apparent if we contrast it with ration lists discovered from the ancient world. These are not without their own difficulties, but they do provide a statistical account of the amounts of food actually paid to individual workers. Second, Broshi and Dar assume that caloric intake is the principal determinant of a healthy diet. This is not the case, as Dauphin rightly observes: "the calorie balance of her diet appears normal, but with a tendency to be on the low side. In reality, it [her diet] was precarious."[4] A diet may contribute sufficient calories for survival but be deficient in vitamins and minerals, with serious consequences for human health. Indeed, as we shall see in chapter 13, a diet consisting of grain, legumes, oil, and figs alone has significant deficiencies.

In light of the limitations of the textual evidence particularly for the early Israelite period, some scholars have sought to use empirical data from archaeological excavations and surveys to model Israelite diet. This empirical data is used to estimate the size of village populations, the amount of land utilized for agricultural purposes, the number of animals that could have been supported, and so forth. The resulting model of the agricultural economy can be used to assess the diet enjoyed in Israelite villages and its nutritional adequacy.

In his survey of Samaria from Iron Age II to the Byzantine period, Dar used historical sources and archaeological evidence to estimate the size of farm holdings and the capacity of the agricultural installations that had been discovered during the survey: wine presses, olive presses, and threshing floors. Unsurprisingly, the archaeological and historical sources are much richer for the later periods, and Dar's results better represent the agricultural possibilities of Roman-Byzantine Samaria.

Dar gives particular attention to Qarawat bene Hassan, a town occupied from the Bronze Age to the present, which appears to have been a significant regional center in the Hellenistic and Roman periods. Dar estimates there to have been around 175 to 200 family holdings that ranged from 8.8 to 10.1 acres. Over half the land was arable, a quarter of which was used for olives and a little less for vines. The public pasturelands to the north of the town amounted to between 330 and 450 acres. Dar calculates that each family could have had a flock with from ten to fifteen animals, as well as one or two head of cattle. Allowing for such resources, Dar is able to give an optimistic account of the diet of the inhabitants of ancient Palestine. The land put to crops was sufficient to provide for the settlement, and thus the cereal was probably grown primarily for local consumption. The production of oil and wine, however, was the most important part of the economy, and the production capacity would appear to have far exceeded local needs. The excess would have been sold at market.[5] The agricultural resources at Qarawat bene Hassan are so generous that it is not surprising that Dar can conclude, not only for the rest of Romano-Byzantine Samaria but also for other historical periods, that "the inhabitants of Palestine enjoyed in ancient times" a "varied and satisfying diet."[6]

Some more complete approaches to modeling, and more directly related to the ancient Israelites, are attempted by Baruch Rosen for the early Iron Age site at Izbet Sartah. In one instance Rosen used the capacity of the silos discovered at Izbet Sartah to calculate the amount of land under cultivation. The number of families at the site allows the number of cattle for plowing to be estimated. Taken together with the animal proportions at the site known from faunal remains, the pattern of animal husbandry can be modeled and the contribution of milk and meat in the human diet determined.[7] Rosen makes allowances for spoiling and the need to keep seed for sowing in the following year. Similarly for the herd numbers, Rosen assumes a cull pattern that would allow the herd to be maintained. The majority of the calories needed by the population of Izbet Sartah would have come from cereals, with protein supplied by legumes. The area under cultivation would have exceeded the villagers' needs, and the surplus could have been exchanged for olive oil, wine, and other foodstuffs. The animal resources were less abundant. Nevertheless, Rosen concludes that this village of a hundred people could have owned around 22 cattle and 130 sheep or goats, and that the village's livestock would have supplied about 0.45 liters of milk and 44 grams of meat per person per day.[8] The population at Izbet Sartah, then, enjoyed a diet that supplied all their calorie, protein, and mineral needs. The only possible deficiency was a lack of vitamin C sources, but Rosen speculates that wild or cultivated greens could have supplied this.[9] On another occasion Rosen worked in the opposite direction. By estimating the population from the size of the buildings, he determined the nutritional needs of the villagers. With this information he can calculate the land under cultivation and the number of animals needed, and determine the feasibility of the local economy.[10]

One significant weakness of Rosen's model lies in its estimation of the animal population. A plausible estimate of the human population can be made from the area of buildings excavated, and an area survey can suggest the amount of land available to a population center. The proportion of caprovines (sheep and goats) to bovines (cows) can be estimated from animal remains, but the number of animals kept by a community must be calculated from these other estimated figures. Aharon Sasson has recently developed a model that incorporates ethnographical data from censuses of Palestine during the British mandate (1923-48). Using the census figures, he calculates the average number of animals per inhabitant for a Palestinian village that is located close to the archaeological site under investigation. In this way calculations of human population also provide an estimate of the animal population. From the number of animals available to a community, Sasson is able to calculate the meat and milk provision per person, the potential area plowed by the cattle, and the level of grain production. Comparing the food production capabilities of a village to the nutritional requirements of its inhabitants can establish the basis of the agricultural economy. He concludes that the villages of Izbet Sartah and Ai had high pastoral components and produced a surplus of grain. The village of Nahal Rephaim, on the other hand, had an economy based on orchards. The grain and animal products generated were for self-consumption and had to be supplemented by trade. Sasson argues that none of the sites produced a surplus in animal products, although they did provide between 30 and 77 grams of meat per person per day and between 149 and 224 milliliters of milk.[11]

The exercise of estimating the amount and type of food consumed in ancient Palestine is valuable, but the figures must be treated with considerable caution, for such models are only as good as the assumptions they make. First, it is possible to develop different models and, consequently, to reach different results. This is aptly demonstrated by examining the two models created by Rosen for the same data. In Rosen's first model the herd is a relatively modest size. There are 120 caprovines and 22 cattle. In Rosen's second model, however, there are 300 caprovines and 12-15 cattle. In this model about the same amount of land is used by the villagers, but a smaller area is devoted to crops.[12] Second, all the data used is estimated on the basis of archaeological evidence or comparative practice: the amount of land worked; the proportion devoted to arable, horticultural, and pastoral use; crop yields; population; and so forth. Not only can individual figures and estimates be disputed, but each figure also introduces a margin of error. These margins of error increase as estimated figures are used together to calculate other figures. Such statistical issues must be taken into account when final figures are adduced. Third, Rosen and Sasson assume that sowing and plowing are the principal inhibitors to more extensive cultivation. However, Halstead has argued that a community's food production capacity is limited by harvesting and postharvest processing. His work suggests that ancient communities could not have harvested cereals at significant levels above that required for subsistence, and certainly not at the levels of surplus demanded by Rosen's and Sasson's models.[13]

Fourth, the estimation of animal numbers remains problematic even in Sasson's modeling. The modern Palestinian villages he examines are considerably larger than the ancient ones, resulting in different farming dynamics. Within these modern villages the number of animals per villager varies from 0.28 to 3.3, that is, by a factor of ten. Animal herders can respond to their environment in numerous ways, and the difference in animal numbers for modern Palestinian villages is a demonstration of that. Fifth, the models of Rosen and Sasson assume that all the cattle are utilized maximally for traction. The potential for this to increase the calculated production of wheat is clear, for the estimated wheat production per person of the Iron Age villages is considerably higher than the figures for wheat production from the Mandate censuses. Izbet Sartah and Ai are estimated to produce 590 and 520 kilograms of wheat per person, but the four twentieth-century villages that Sasson examines could produce only between 50 and 175 kilograms of wheat per person.

Sixth, the analyses undertaken by Rosen and Sasson assume that all meat is consumed within the village and none of it is exchanged for other commodities. This is a puzzling assumption when set alongside the idea that some villages aimed to generate a grain surplus that could be traded. Thus, the models appear to be working with an idea of subsistence or trade in a manner that is not consistent or whose logic is unexplained. Animal remains from excavations are assumed to be representative of the diet consumed, with an identity between producers and consumers. However, when a surplus of crops is produced by the calculations, it is assumed that crops are traded out of the population circle. It is possible, then, that the utilization of animal products, including important proteins, vitamins, and minerals, within the villages has been overestimated. Sasson appears to assume that, since their own animals would only just meet the animal protein needs of the community, the animals cannot have been traded outside. This assumes the precedence of dietary need over any political or economic constraints that may have existed. Additionally, it is more likely that animals will be marketed than grain, since cereals are difficult to transport and have a relatively low value. If wheat and barley were traded, it would have been economically viable only within a small area. Animals, however, are not only a valuable resource with their products highly prized, but are also easily driven to another district. Seventh, all models calculate the production capabilities of the whole village and then the figure per person. This assumes an equal division of fields, labor, and animals, or an equitable distribution of agricultural produce. This criticism, together with the preceding one, is particularly significant since what is assumed is a certain understanding of early Israelite society that is not uncontested. Unexpressed is the view that early Israelite society was essentially egalitarian and that very little trade existed between or within districts.[14]

What such models show at their best is the probable way land was utilized in different locations in Palestine in response to different environmental niches. We should not be surprised that in an average year the Israelite villages had access to sufficient agricultural resources, and that for certain products the village could not only supply its own needs, but also produce a trading surplus. As we will see in the following two chapters, the environmental and climatic challenges required the Israelites to produce a surplus in "average" years. Dar, Rosen, and Sasson also show, as David Hopkins has argued elsewhere, that most villages in the Israelite highlands would have had a mixed farming strategy, so minimalizing their risk.[15] What these models are not able to provide, it seems to me, are conclusive arguments about the nature and sufficiency of the Israelite diet.

CHAPTER 8

Environment and Climate

Questions of food consumption cannot be detached from basic questions of environment and climate, since these affect all aspects of food production, including the level of supply. The constituent elements of a region's diet may in principle be healthy and nutritious, but if there is not sufficient supply, some or all of the inhabitants will suffer from malnutrition. It is not possible to think of the environment and climate of Israel in absolute terms, because there is a symbiotic relationship between human society and environment. The physical environment of Palestine has been manipulated by human societies from the very beginning. Indeed, agriculture is in its very essence the manipulation of the natural environment for the purpose of producing plants and rearing livestock for maximum human utility. By the time the Israelites settled Canaan, for example, the landscape already bore the marks of millennia of human activity, and was quite different from its "natural" state. Nevertheless, the environment places certain limitations on human activities, as we are aware in the present, but this was much more the case in ancient times, and therefore can to some degree be considered as an element independent of human society. Human societies, on the other hand, cannot be considered apart from the environment they inhabit. The environment sets limitations and demands on human activity that societies change in response to. Some areas are inhospitable to human settlement while in others humans can flourish. Other areas, as we will see, lie between these two extremes and can be marginal for human survival.

Our discussion of environmental factors will be relatively brief and will focus on issues most pertinent to food production and diet. An important factor in determining Palestine's food production possibilities is its geology. This includes not only the shape of the land, but also the presence of water resources and soil formation. Since George Adam Smith's *Historical Geography of the Holy Land,* it has been common to consider the land of Israel as a series of strips beginning with the coastal plain in the west and ending with the Jordanian desert in the east (see map 3).[1] We will follow that time-honored approach in describing the environment of ancient Palestine.

We begin, then, with the Mediterranean coast. The coastal plain extends along the length of Palestine, broken only where the Mount Carmel mountain range juts into the Mediterranean Sea. This area was rarely controlled by the Israelites. In the north of Palestine it is very narrow, and in ancient times a number of marshy areas probably restricted communications and agriculture. In the south the plain of Sharon gradually broadens out into the area dominated by the five cities of Ashdod, Ashkelon, Ekron, Gath, and Gaza, the so-called Philistine pentapolis. The smooth topography of the coastal plain allows for easy cultivation, although low rainfall, especially in the south, limits agricultural possibilities. In the Iron Age this area was probably used primarily for cereal growing, with some horticulture. In the north the principal crop would have been wheat, giving way to more barley farther south as annual rainfall diminishes. Between the Philistine plain and the southern highlands of Israel is the half-strip known as the Shephelah. These valleys and low-lying hills are dominated by rendzina soils, which have a high lime content and are agriculturally fairly poor.

The Palestinian highlands — Galilee, the Samaria Hills, and the Judean Hills — run north to south in the center of the country. In the first half of the first millennium b.c. they made up the heartland of the Israelite kingdoms. The dominant soil of these areas is terra rosa. This fertile soil is suitable for crops, though its clayey texture makes cultivation difficult and it requires continuous treatment to be suitable for agricultural exploitation. It is frequently shallow and stony, though in places the soil is deep enough and the landscape sufficiently smooth to be given over to cereals. On the slopes the soil is easily eroded, and in the Iron Age this susceptibility to erosion was managed through terracing. When terraced, the slopes could be devoted to olive and vine cultivation. Less common in the highlands is Mediterranean brown forest soil. It too is a fertile soil, but it occurs

in areas of smoother topography than terra rosa, allowing easier exploitation. In the eastern parts of Galilee a basaltic soil is found, but the existence
of many boulders restricts utilization of this fertile soil. Between the Samaria Hills and Galilee the highland backbone is broken by the Jezreel Valley. Here the alluvial soils and flat topography offer some of the best opportunities for cultivation, although some areas, particularly in the west,
would have been too marshy in ancient times. In the south the Judean Hills
give way to the Negev, where low rainfall and desert soils offer limited opportunities for cultivation.

The central highland belt drops away sharply to the east, and the landscape makes its way down toward the Jordan River. This area is in the rain
shadow of the highlands, and its dry climate offers limited opportunities
for cultivation, especially in the south of the country. The Jordan Valley
makes a sharp incision between the Israelite highlands and the Transjordan plateau, running north to south from the Huleh Valley to Galilee
before ending at the Dead Sea. The alluvial soil alongside the Jordan can
offer some good opportunities for cultivation, though these diminish toward the Dead Sea. On the other side of the Jordan the Transjordanian plateau rises high above the river valley. In the north — biblical Bashan —
crops can be grown on the fertile soil. The area around Gilead was heavily
forested in ancient times, but could support not only grain but also olives
and vines. Farther south the decreasing rainfall restricts land use to mixed
cereal and animal husbandry.[2]

This broad characterization of the geology and soil structure of Palestine as it concerns food production must be modified by the diversity of
Palestine's environment that results in distinctive microenvironments.[3] It
is evident that the environment of Palestine places various constraints on
human agricultural and pastoral activities according to location. This diversity is reflected in Thomas L. Thompson's analysis of the agricultural
strategies of the early Iron Age inhabitants of the central highlands: "From
its earliest period, settlement in the central hills seems to have involved a
threefold economy . . . namely, animal husbandry on the eastern fringe,
grain agriculture and field crops in the central heartland, and horticulture
along the rugged southwestern slopes."[4] These constraints together with
the diversity of Palestine mean there can be no single model of Israelite
food production, and consequently, talk of a single Israelite diet is somewhat misleading. The existence of trade will increase the uniformity of
consumption patterns. However, it will not entirely erase the differences,

for most food was produced for self-consumption and some goods, such as cereals, could not be traded beyond the local area for economic or practical reasons.

The Israelite highlands are the area for which language of the "typical Israelite diet" might appropriately serve. This is the "Israel" most commonly represented on the pages of the Old Testament. The hills and valleys provide land that is more or less serviceable for agriculture, although some areas are rocky or have only a thin soil. Land use was principally devoted to vines and olives, wheat and barley. As Thompson indicates, specialization could have been pursued in the central and northern highland areas and the Jezreel Valley. Toward the south and east, lower and more variable rainfall would have encouraged a mixed farming, an agro-pastoralism,[5] with the proportion of barley to wheat increasing as rainfall decreased. This, of course, is the agricultural landscape of the Judean Highlands, the region familiar to the Jerusalem elite who played an important role in the composition and editing of the biblical books. In the Negev to the south and the Judean desert to the east, cereal cultivation gave way to pastoralism. Those who shepherded flocks were not self-sufficient, but lived in economic relationship with those who cultivated crops. For most of Transjordan vine and olive cultivation was not possible and the land would have been devoted to cereals and livestock. Again, as one moved south, the land would have been increasingly given over to grazing.

The climate of Palestine, however, is perhaps the most significant constraint on agriculture in Palestine, and consequently on the availability of sufficient food. The most important factor is the quantity and distribution of rainfall. This fact was appreciated by the Israelites:

> If you will only heed his every commandment that I am commanding you today — loving YHWH your God and serving him with all your heart and with all your soul — then he will give the rain for your land in its season, the early rain and the later rain, and you will gather in your grain, your wine and your oil; and he will give grass in your fields for your livestock, and you will eat your fill. Take care, or you will be seduced into turning away, serving other gods and worshiping them, for then the anger of YHWH will be kindled against you and he will shut up the heavens, so that there will be no rain and the land will yield no fruit; then you will perish quickly off the good land that YHWH is giving you. (Deut. 11:13-17)

Understanding the impact of the climate upon agriculture and, consequently, food production is therefore an important task.

Accurate recording of climatic variation has been possible only in modern times, and consequently historical records contribute to our understanding of the climate of ancient Palestine only in a very limited way. Scientific reconstruction of historical climatic variation is an extremely difficult area, but one that can increasingly be taken into account.[6] In broad terms, major changes to the climate of Palestine have not occurred in the last ten thousand years.[7] But minor climatic variations have had significant implications for certain communities, especially those in marginal agricultural areas such as the Negev highlands.[8] It is thus possible to use our knowledge of the present climate of Palestine and meteorological measurements of a century or so to assess the probable effect of climate on Israelite agriculture, but we shall need to bear in mind that the aridity line — the boundary between regions capable of marginal agriculture and those capable only of pastoralism — may have varied from its present position. Indeed, it may have varied during the Iron Age.

The principal characteristic of Palestinian climate is the division of the year into two seasons: hot and dry summers, cool and wet winters. During the summer a large area of low pressure stretches across south Asia and East Africa, resulting in clear skies and hot days. The months from May until September are almost completely rainless. During the winter a shift in the location of the temperate and subtropical belts results in a constant series of cyclonic weather systems that pass over Israel from west to east bringing heavy bursts of rain. The path of these weather systems can vary, with more moving across the north of the Levant. Consequently a smaller number of these cyclonic systems pass over the south of the country.

A consequence of the paths taken by these weather systems is that Palestine has a distinctive distribution of rainfall. In general terms the farther north, the greater the rainfall. Thus Galilee boasts an average rainfall of over 700 millimeters, while in the Judean and Samarian highlands it is more like 400-550 millimeters per annum. As you move farther south and east, average annual rainfall continues to decrease, with the Judean desert and the Negev receiving less than 200 millimeters. In these arid regions cereal crops would have been cultivatable only in exceptional years and the land would have been used only as pasture.

Bare statistics about average rainfall can be misleading, for variation also makes a significant difference, particularly in the semiarid regions of

Palestine. The northerly bias of the cyclonic systems means not only that annual rainfall decreases as one moves south, but also that variability increases. "Distance from the normal track of depressions also determines rainfall variability since the closer the distance the more likely an area is to receive rain from at least a portion of a passing storm."[9] D. Sharon has analyzed rainfall variation in Palestine on the basis of records from the last hundred years. His findings show the Galilean highlands to have a standard deviation of between 20 and 25 percent of the average rainfall, the Samarian and Judean highlands between 25 and 35 percent, the Shephelah between 35 and 40 percent, and the Negev over 40 percent.[10] Hopkins summarizes the significance of this variability: "For Jerusalem this means that three years out of ten will experience accumulation of rainfall about 16 percent less than the mean and that one or two of these years will experience more than 25 percent less."[11]

The variability of the rainfall, and its consequences for agriculture, was recognized in ancient times. In the Babylonian Talmud Rabbi Eleazer ben Perata is attributed with saying, "From the day the Temple was destroyed the rains have become irregular in the world. There is a year which has abundant rains, and there is a year with but little rain. There is a year in which the rains come down in their proper season and a year in which they come out of season. . . . In the period of the Second Temple the rains came on time and as a result the crops were of a far better quality."[12] The irregularity of the rainfall and the low level of rainfall in the south of Palestine — the Judean Hills, the Shephelah, and the Negev — produce a significant risk of crop failure or diminished yield. Provided a dry year is followed by a good year, the risk could be significantly moderated by stored grain. However, the rainfall is so variable, especially in the south of the country, that two consecutive dry years are not improbable. Twice in the period from 1920 to 1960 Jerusalem endured two or more consecutive dry years.[13]

Annual rainfall is not the only climatic factor that can impact agriculture in Israel, and consequently food production and consumption. As is apparent from Deuteronomy 11, the timely appearance of the "early rains" and "later rains" is also important. The Deuteronomic text is easily misunderstood to imply that the wet season consisted of two rainy periods at the beginning and the end of winter with a dry period between.[14] In fact, "all the figures show that the rainfall tends to get steadily greater toward the middle of the season and then to decrease again."[15] The "early rains" mark the beginning of the wet season, and the time for plowing and sowing. If they do not appear on time, but come later, the crops do not fully mature before they need to be harvested. The "later rains" are the continuation of the wet season until April. If the wet season ends prematurely — in biblical parlance, before the later rains — the crops may be stunted. Historical climate data for Jerusalem shows how frequent such potentially disastrous occurrences are: 20 percent of the time there is a dry late season, 13 percent of the time there is a dry early season, and 2 to 3 percent of the time the rain is compressed into a very short season. In the north of the country a dry early season is less likely (6 percent), but a dry late season is far more common (31 percent).[16] In other words, three or four years in every ten have an irregular pattern of rain that carries significant implications for crop yields. In these situations the farmer can modify the effects of the vicissitudes of the weather to some degree. For example, since seed is not sown until the onset of the rain, the farmer can vary the amount of land devoted to particular crops, as still occurs in modern Jordan.[17] Nevertheless, the farmer can hope only to mitigate what could potentially be a disastrous season.

Crop yields could also be negatively affected by disease and animals. The biblical depictions of the catastrophic consequences of a locust swarm, for example in the book of Joel, are justly well known. In the curses at the end of the book of Deuteronomy, the destruction of the Mediterranean triad is envisaged through pestilence. "You shall carry much seed into the field but shall gather little in, for the locust shall consume it. You shall plant vineyards and dress them, but you shall neither drink the wine nor gather the grapes, for the worm shall eat them. You shall have olive trees throughout all your territory, but you shall not anoint yourselves with oil, for your olives shall drop off" (Deut. 28:38-40). Rainfall variability was probably the most significant cause of diminished harvests, but pests and disease added an additional uncertainty, and without modern pesticides the ancient Israelite farmer would have been helpless in the face of such adversity.

CHAPTER 9

Food Shortage and Famine

There are good grounds for believing, then, that malnourishment was something that many Israelites would have experienced at some point during their lives. This is demonstrated by the appearance of famine in the biblical writings. It is not possible to come to any firm conclusions about the historicity of any of the particular famines described in the biblical texts. Nevertheless, the motif of famine is used frequently enough that we can conclude it was a far from irregular experience for the Israelites. In the words of Aharoni, "years of drought and famine run like a scarlet thread through the ancient history of Palestine."[1] Famines and food shortages did not result only from droughts; they could also be caused by social and political events, especially warfare. Numerous biblical texts indicate that the realities of ancient warfare included plundering food supplies or destroying agricultural resources (for example, Judg. 6:1-6). Besieged cities were brought to submission by cutting off their water supply or through starvation.

In the narrative literature of the Old Testament, famine frequently functions to enforce the movement of significant characters from one place to another. Thus, famine causes the patriarchs to move outside the Promised Land in search of food (Gen. 12; 26; 42), Naomi and her family to move to Moab (Ruth 1), and Elijah to seek refuge in Phoenicia (1 Kings 17). In Deuteronomy and the prophetic literature famine is often used as one of God's covenant curses. When the Israelites rebel and turn from their God, he will punish them by suspending the rain, thus bringing famine on the land. In the postbiblical period too there is evidence for the vulnerability of the land to poor harvests and crop failure.[2] Josephus provides detailed accounts of severe famines around the time of Christ. One in the reign of Herod the Great lasted two years (24-23 B.C.); another occurred in the reign of Claudius (A.D. 46 or 47). In both cases famine relief was brought through royal intervention.[3] On the basis of the rabbinic writings, Sperber observed that "the incidence of famine was a very common phenomenon in the later third century."[4] The vulnerability of the food economy in Israel is also seen in rabbinic actions to forbid certain food items from being exported.[5]

The biblical accounts cannot tell us about the frequency of the famines, nor about their extent and seriousness. In an important work on famine and food supply in the Greco-Roman world, Peter Garnsey distinguishes between famine, food shortage, and endemic hunger.[6] "*Famine*," he writes elsewhere, "is a critical shortage of essential foodstuffs, leading through hunger to a substantially increased mortality rate in a community or region, and involving a collapse of the social, political and moral order"; "*food shortage* is a short-term reduction in the amount of available foodstuffs, as indicated by rising prices, popular discontent and hunger, in the worst cases leading to death by disease or starvation"; and "endemic hunger, or chronic malnutrition, is a condition of long term food deprivation."[7] These are important observations for at least two reasons. First, it is common to collapse food shortage into famine. In the terms of Garnsey's definition, famine is a genuine catastrophe that is relatively rare. "Food shortages" fall short of these and have varying degrees of seriousness. Second, such distinctions help us recognize the importance of endemic malnutrition as a significant problem in preindustrial societies outside of specific instances of famine or food shortage. In other words, genuine famine may have occurred only once or twice in a lifetime, and food shortages a little more often. However, some vulnerable parts of society may have experienced chronic malnutrition as a regular feature of their lives.

The failure to make such distinctions and give serious reflection to the problem of food shortage is found in the work of Dar. As part of his arguments against an earlier generation of scholars who believed the Israelites had a poor diet, he writes, "only in times of widespread starvation caused by a lengthy drought and wars did people die from lack of food in parts of Palestine and Syria. In the time of King Herod such a famine resulted from three years of drought. Josephus tells us that the problem was solved by importing grain from neighbouring Egypt."[8] This fails to take into account that starvation and death are only the most extreme forms of malnutrition. The absence of significant mortality due to lack of food is not evidence of a satisfying and nutritious diet nor that malnutrition was not a significant problem in the population. The ability of a powerful monarch like Herod to resolve the problem to some degree — and probably only for some of the population — in one particular instance does not allow us to ignore food shortage as a recurring and significant problem in the ancient economy of Palestine.

For the majority of ancient Israelites severe food shortages or famines would probably have been episodic. Nevertheless, an insufficient diet for a temporary period could have significant and disproportionate health implications, especially for certain sectors of the population, such as pregnant or lactating mothers, and children. Physical starvation would have been an unusual extreme, brought about by a combination of circumstances, but for a child or woman weakened by hunger, illness could bring an early death. Those who survived would have remained more susceptible to disease for the rest of their lives. For a much smaller number of Israelites, those who were very poor either because they were landless or socially dislocated, malnourishment would have been ever on the horizon. Were food to be in short supply generally, the outlook for these members of society would have been bleak indeed.

Various strategies were employed to reduce the likelihood of food shortages and to cope with them when they occurred. Storage facilities would have been large enough to store surplus crops from a good harvest. Where possible, risk was spread through practicing mixed farming. Were one crop to fail, then other crops or livestock could be eaten or traded for food. Thus wheat and barley could be grown, and although the latter could be used for fodder, it was usually cultivated for human consumption.[9]

More drastic strategies may have been employed by the population during famines or by the poor during food shortages. We have already observed that migration was a strategy familiar to the biblical writers. Leaving your own land and society is high risk and must have been pursued only in extreme cases. Another possibility is to extend the foods consumed. Barley has already been mentioned, as has foraging for wild foods (cf. 2 Kings 4; Job 30:3-4). Substitute foods must do in times of shortage. Thus, in Ezekiel 4:9 the prophet bakes a cake made of a variety of ingredients as a demonstration of the siege conditions that Jerusalem will soon suffer.[10] The results may not have been especially palatable, but would be more nutritious than some of the other "fillers," such as chaff and straw, that people may have resorted to during famine conditions.[11] A disagreeable menu item would have been the donkey's head being sold for food in 2 Kings 6 during the famine of Samaria. In the later dietary laws the donkey was forbidden as a food, and a head would have provided only some usable meat. In the same siege the biblical historian also tells of two mothers consuming their children. Other accounts of cannibalism can be found in Lamentations 2:20 and 4:10 (cf. Deut. 28:52-57; Ezek. 5:10). The possibility that human flesh was consumed in extreme circumstances cannot be entirely discounted. We should, though, treat such texts with considerable caution, for accounts of cannibalism in other cultures are often used for polemical effect and cannot be taken as dispassionate reportage.[12]

CHAPTER 10

The Consumption of Meat:
Archaeological Evidence

In the second century B.C., the Jewish sage Ben Sira wrote, "the basic necessities of human life are water and fire and iron and salt and wheat flour and milk and honey, the blood of the grape and oil and clothing" (Ecclus. 39:26). It has often been observed that a striking omission from this list is meat. For many Old Testament scholars of the last hundred years, this is not surprising, since most agree that "people of ordinary circumstances ate meat only rarely."[1] One of the purposes of many of the models we examined in chapter 7 is to challenge this assumption in biblical scholarship. It is not surprising, then, that one of the results that Dar, Rosen, and Sasson provide in their models is an estimation of the amount of meat available per head of population of the examined villages per day. As a result Dar can claim that "it used to be commonly thought that the inhabitants of the eastern Mediterranean basin did not eat much meat in ancient times. But the most recent excavations do not support this theory."[2] Since meat provides a number of valuable vitamins, proteins, and minerals, this would go some way to establishing Dar's claim about "the varied and satisfying diet which the inhabitants of Palestine enjoyed in ancient times." It is clear, then, that the issue of meat consumption in Israel demands further examination.

We will examine the question in two stages. First, we will consider what can be known from the archaeological evidence. As we have already noted, bones are by far the most common discovery during archaeological excavations. Consequently it is now possible to produce a nuanced picture of the consumption of meat across ancient Palestine from the middle of the second millennium to the middle of the first millennium B.C. Nevertheless, as insightful as this picture is, it cannot give us decisive information about *how much* meat was consumed by individual ancient Israelites. Animal bones may be the most common archaeological find, but it is impossible to tell how many people ate the meat and over what period they ate it. For this reason it will be necessary to consider, in the next chapter, some of the anthropological parallels for meat consumption before turning, in the following chapter, to the question of distribution.

Factors Determining Animal Husbandry in Ancient Israel

The remains of animals recovered from an archaeological site can, with modern scientific methods, provide various information about the animals kept and the uses of them by human beings. Recovered bones can be identified in order to provide figures for the relative proportions of animals at a site.[3] Long bones and teeth evidence the maturity of an animal and can be used to calculate the approximate age at which the animal was killed. In sites where a significant number of bones are found, a profile of the kill-off pattern can be determined.[4] With information about animal proportions and kill-off pattern, a picture of the agricultural strategies at a site can be sketched. This is because animals are not just the sum of the meat they provide, but are also exploited for a number of secondary products.

The caprovines — sheep and goats — are the most common species discovered in archaeological excavations in Palestine. It is not always possible to distinguish between sheep and goats because of the close relationship between the two species.[5] Where this can be done the goals of the herders can be perceived. Sheep are preferred for their wool and also for their milk. Goats, on the other hand, are better suited to more arid environments and breed more quickly than sheep. Goats also provide more milk than sheep and for a longer period.[6]

The strategies of goat herders and shepherds are also evidenced by the kill-off patterns at a site. The initial model developed by Payne distinguished three different patterns depending on the primary output being pursued.[7] For wool production a large proportion of the animals survive into adulthood, including the males, most of which are castrated. Selective culling may take place to maximize the use of pasture, but otherwise animals are culled only when annual wool production begins to diminish. In a dairy herd very young animals, especially the males, are culled to maximize the milk available to the herder. The females and a few males are kept until adulthood for breeding and milk production. Where meat production is the primary output, most of the animals are culled before reaching adulthood. This maximizes the weight gain in relation to the herder's investment. An additional factor is the common preference for tender young meat, although this cannot be assumed for the Middle East where there is a widespread preference for fatty portions. In practice, Payne suggests, a herder or shepherd may choose not to focus on one output, but to pursue a mixed strategy.

Since Payne's initial work a number of important modifications to his models have been developed. Redding demonstrated that outputs were often subordinated to herd security. In ancient societies the herd was a long-term investment not only for the herder but also for his entire family. Consequently short-term gains were sacrificed for the long-term maintenance of the herd.[8] Cribb showed that seeking to maximize milk production would also result in efficient production in meat and wool.[9] In addition, he confirmed Redding's observation about the importance of herd security, noting that flock growth was often important in herding strategies.[10] Wapnish and Hesse have highlighted the fact that each of these models assumes a subsistence economy — in other words, that the finds at a site represent a closed system where producers are also consumers. If, however, animals are being sent to market outside the community, this will affect not only patterns of production but also the nature of finds at archaeological sites. In particular, kill-off patterns will differ markedly depending on whether a site is orientated toward the production of animals or their consumption.[11] An urban society that is primarily involved in consumption rather than production will be evidenced by a reduced selection of cuts and a bias toward animals at particular ages. Conversely, a production economy will have an absence of animals at a prime age.

Cattle were exploited for two main reasons: most importantly they provided traction for plowing the fields, and secondarily they were a source of meat. Although cows are associated with milk production in the Western world, this was not their primary association in the ancient Near East. Cattle were the preferred animals for plowing. Horses were too rare and valuable to be used for this task, plus their use for traction was a later European innovation. The donkey was a common beast of burden, and while it could be used to pull a plow, it was not as strong or as steady as an ox. Cattle were also a significant contributor of meat because of their size. Thus, although caprovines outnumbered cattle at the majority of Iron Age sites in Palestine, cattle frequently contributed more meat.[12] Assessment of the age of cattle can indicate how they were being utilized. A high rate of survival into adulthood suggests use for traction, while a significant culling by the age of three and a half indicates use for meat.

Pigs, unlike caprovines and cattle, have no secondary products, and are exploited solely for their meat. They breed far more quickly than the other domesticated animals, and although they cannot eat grass, they can be fed on many other things, including waste. They also have a high fat and calorie content. The lack of secondary exploitation means that most pig remains are from young animals slaughtered for meat.

The relative frequency of domesticated animals at a site is therefore affected by a number of factors. First, the natural environment places certain constraints on the animals that are kept. Cattle and caprovines need adequate pasture, while pigs need shade and wallow. Goats are best suited to some of the arid areas found in the eastern and southern parts of Palestine. Israel, as we have seen, had a number of environmental niches. Successful animal exploitation would have reflected these realities, and herding strategies would have varied from place to place. Second, the exploitation of the natural environment by human beings can take on numerous different forms determined by the dynamic interaction of producers and consumers. The composition of herds can result from the decision of the herders, the demands of the market, and the intervention of central authorities. This can occur for complex and sometimes unconscious reasons. When a community moves toward agricultural intensification, for example, the number of cattle generally increases and the number of caprovines decreases. Such changing patterns of animal utilization can be seen in ancient Palestine as seminomadic groups take up settled agriculture. The reasons for pig husbandry are still poorly understood, but are associated with such disparate purposes as demand for meat, nonintense agriculture, and moves toward economic independence.[13]

The particular patterns of animal husbandry that result from these complex interactions of human beings with their society and their physical environment cannot be easily summarized. This is true even for an area as small as Palestine during the Iron Age. The environmental constraints vary considerably from one end of Palestine to the other. Similarly the political and social situation in Palestine changed dramatically during the period from the Israelite settlement of the land around 1200 B.C. to the end of the Persian period in 322 B.C. A decentralized tribal society gave way to a monarchy and finally to a subordinate state or province within a vast empire. Consequently, we will need to examine animal husbandry in specific instances and map how it varies across space and time. Our ability to map the practices is constrained by the snapshots of animal consumption at those sites where significant excavations have taken place and produced sizable samples of animal bones.[14]

Animal Utilization Prior to the Iron Age

The Israelite tribes that appeared in Palestine at some point at the beginning of the Iron Age were heirs to long-established patterns of agriculture and animal husbandry in the Levant. There were no significant changes to the animals that were kept or to the practices and technology of husbandry. Israel's practices were not unique, but belong within the broad context of the history of animal husbandry in Palestine. Whatever assessment is made about settlement patterns and people movements, agriculturally speaking, the Iron Age was part of a continually evolving relationship between human beings, their animals, and their environment.

The Late Bronze Age period (ca. 1500-1200 B.C.) that preceded the Iron Age was marked by severe demographic crises resulting in complex changes to the settlement pattern of ancient Palestine. The exact significance of these changes is still a matter of considerable debate among scholars. In the central highlands some towns and villages appear to have been abandoned, with the remaining towns and villages shrinking in size. On the other hand, some of the settlements from the Middle Bronze Age continued to flourish, and along the coast new settlements were founded, nourished by marine trade.

In a detailed examination of husbandry practices from the Middle Bronze Age to the Late Bronze Age, Horwitz and Milevski have observed that even at sites where there was continuity of occupation, there were significant changes in agricultural strategies.[15] Agriculture intensified in urban centers along the coast, as seen in a relative increase in cattle alongside a relative decrease in goats and pigs. This intensified agricultural activity might represent the response of lowland urban societies to the period of economic instability that characterized the end of the Bronze Age. As Lev-Tov suggests was the case at Ekron, this may have been a conscious move toward a more self-sufficient economy.[16] The economic instability of the period is also evidenced in a marked increase in the consumption of wild animals. This is one of the ways a community can increase its utilization of local resources. Another possible explanation of the agricultural intensification, according to Horwitz and Milevski, is increasing economic demands from the Egyptian empire.

The case of the sites in the highlands is more difficult to assess. At Manahat and Shiloh, significant changes in animal husbandry do not seem to have occurred. Both sites evidence a pastoralist economy that is maintained from the Middle Bronze Age into the Late Bronze Age. It has often been suggested that a widespread turn to pastoralism occurred in the highlands during the Late Bronze Age. Unfortunately, with our current state of knowledge, this suggestion cannot be confirmed with any certainty.[17]

Animal Utilization in Iron Age I

The beginning of Iron Age I (1200-1000 B.C.) has usually been taken to mark the beginning of the Israelite period. The main location of Israelite groups in this period is in the central highlands. In this region there continued to be a strong preference for caprovines. This tendency is increasingly in evidence in the south of the highlands and also in settlements in the Negev where the arid environment is poorly suited to cattle and pigs.[18] At sites such as Jerusalem, Ai, and Raddana caprovines contribute from 80 to 90 percent of the animal bones. The remaining material is primarily cattle, which contributes from 10 to 15 percent. This low level of cattle suggests an economy focused around pastoral activities rather than the growth of cereals.[19] The exceptions to this are the sites at Mount Ebal and Shiloh in the center of the country, where around 22 percent of the animal remains are cattle. Since both places were important cultic sites at the time, the appearance of more cattle may well be evidence of sacrificial preferences rather than typical animal proportions for the surrounding areas.[20]

Highland sites generally show a preference for goats, although some sites have almost equal numbers of goats and sheep.[21] This stands in marked contrast to the coastal plain, where there is a strong preference for sheep. Unsurprisingly, finds from the low foothills of the Shephelah suggest a mediatory position with equal numbers of goats and sheep. The kill-off patterns for the highland sites show that the majority of animals reached adulthood. The animal economy of the highland would appear, therefore, to be strongly orientated toward nonmeat, or secondary, production. The preference for goats suggests that the animals were being exploited primarily for dairy products. An alternative explanation has been proposed by Hesse, who argues that there is evidence of a cull pattern at Ai and Raddana consistent with a production center in a market economy.[22] Higher numbers of sheep would have been kept, but these would have been sold in urban centers, probably located on the coast, for meat. The goats would have provided milk and, at the end of their productive lives, meat for the rural economy.

The foothills of the Shephelah show evidence of intensive agriculture. At Tel Harrasim only 58 percent of the animal bones were from caprovines, while almost 30 percent came from cattle. At Izbet Sartah cattle accounted for 34 percent of the animal bones.[23] This suggests a typical mixed agriculture with dry farming as the mainstay of the economy, supplemented by animal husbandry.[24]

The sites in the highlands and the Shephelah show a very low level of pig exploitation in the early Iron Age. Since these correspond to the areas where the Israelite kingdoms would later flourish, it is frequently argued that the lack of pig remains at a site is an important cultural marker of a Hebrew population.[25] Specialist archaeozoologists are less convinced, not least because a great number of factors have been offered to explain the presence or absence of pig husbandry.[26] It is not clear that one factor — a pig taboo among a certain ethnic group — should be given explanatory priority in the case of highland settlements in the Iron Age. Pig exploitation was never especially common in the ancient Near East, and had been in steady decline during the Bronze Age.

A quite different pattern of animal exploitation prevailed on the coastal plain, including a striking utilization of the pig. The excavations at Ekron show a dramatic increase in the consumption of pig during the early Iron Age, a change usually associated with the arrival of the Philistines in the area.[27] A number of explanations have been given for the popularity of the pig among the Philistine population. It is possible that pig husbandry was practiced in the Aegean areas from which the Philistines migrated, and that it was a vestige from this earlier period from which the Philistines eventually divested. An alternative suggestion is that pigs make a very good husbandry strategy for new settlers, because they breed quickly. Whatever the exact reasons, a high level of pig consumption at a site along the coastal plain in this period probably indicates a Philistine presence. The absence of pigs, however, cannot be taken as evidence of an Israelite population. Not only might the site just as easily be occupied by one of the many other peoples who dwelt in Palestine at the time, but also some locations known to be Philistine settlements, such as Tell Qasile and Tell Jemmeh, had a low level of pig consumption.[28] Even at Ekron pig remains peaked at 24 percent of the animal bones, before pig exploitation declined rapidly so that by Iron Age II pigs accounted for less than 4 percent of the bones at the site. Thus, pig husbandry at Philistine sites was not universal and was relatively short-lived.

Even at the sites on the coastal plain where pigs were an important constituent of the local economy, caprovines and cattle were still the dominant species. The relative frequency of each species can be quite different from the highland areas. At Ekron caprovines account for only 43 percent of the animal remains, with cattle accounting for 36 percent. Although the proportion of sheep and goats fluctuates, there is a preference for sheep.[29] The age at which the animals were culled suggests that secondary exploitation was important, sheep for wool rather than milk, and cattle for traction. Some of the cattle were also culled young for meat, and the goats may also have been exploited primarily for meat.[30] Farther down the coastal plain at Tell Jemmeh, caprovines dominated, with around four sheep to one goat. The high level of sheep exploitation suggests the importance of wool production for the local economy. The low level of cattle at this site is perhaps due to the arid environment. Animal exploitation at Tell Jemmeh does not change significantly from the Middle Bronze Age through to the Persian period, despite increased cattle use elsewhere in the coastal plain.[31] Thus, with the exception of a site like Tell Jemmeh near the aridity line, the coastal plain had an agricultural economy. This formed a strong contrast with the pastoral economies of the central highlands.

Animal Utilization in Iron Age II

Few changes are apparent in the animal economies of the highland area during the second part of the Iron Age (1000-550 B.C.). Slightly more cattle appear, but caprovines still dominate. The animals are still used predominantly for secondary products, but there is evidence of a slight increase in the number of animals butchered at prime ages.[32] This would suggest that the consumption of animals played a more important role in herding strategies than was the case in earlier periods. Similar patterns are found in the Negev, where about 10-15 percent of the animal bones are from cattle and 75-85 percent are from caprovines. At Tel Masos the settlement was poorer, and the small sample indicates husbandry focused on caprovine herding.[33]

In the Shephelah cattle continue to be an important part of the economy. At Tel Harrasim the kill-off patterns suggest that cattle were exploited to a greater degree for meat than they had been in Iron Age I. At Lachish too cattle were increasingly exploited for meat. Nevertheless, in both cases the majority of cattle still survived until maturity and were used primarily for traction. Caprovines were also kept increasingly for meat at Tel Harrasim, but with a secondary focus on milk and wool. At Lachish, however, evidence shows not only that the number of sheep increased but also that most of them were being kept until maturity. This probably suggests wool production.

An emphasis on wool is more strongly demonstrated on the coastal plain where the Philistine towns of Ekron and Tell Jemmeh show an increase in sheep production. As a result, cattle make up a smaller percentage of the overall animal population than we might have expected from earlier periods.[34] Tel Hamid and Ashkelon also show a very high level of sheep exploitation.[35] The data from Ashkelon is surprising since it shows cattle contributing only 8 percent of the bones found. The explanation for this is uncertain, but the overall level of cattle remains consistent into the Persian period.[36] The shift toward intensive wool production is very marked, then, on the coastal plain, but is consistent with trends from the early Iron Age. Wapnish questions whether wool production alone can explain all these changes. In her opinion the kill-off patterns during the Assyrian period show a shift toward mature animals that is unsustainable as a pastoral strategy unless animals in their prime were being outsourced. She suggests that this might have resulted either from market opportunity or from Assyrian tribute demands.[37] Since other aspects of the Palestinian economy were being exploited by the Assyrian overlords at this time, this suggestion may well be correct.

In the north of Israel, three neighboring sites on the edge of the Jezreel Valley have produced sizable faunal samples. The animal profiles demonstrate how quite different strategies can be followed within a short distance.[38] At Tell Qiri there is evidence of a mixed economy with some cattle but a high level of caprovines, with an equal number of sheep and goats. The position of the site on the edge of the Carmel Mountains perhaps explains the pastoralist tendency.[39] At Tel Yoqne'am, the main urban center of the region, caprovines are still the most common animal remains discovered, but the level of cattle is higher, which suggests dry farming was pursued.[40] The utilization of cattle is far greater, however, at Tel Qashish, another small village at the floor of the valley a few kilometers away, where almost half of the animal remains are cattle. Among caprovines there is a strong preference for goats.[41] Each of the sites has a high level of immature-animal slaughter, suggesting exploitation for meat and milk. The highest level is at Tel Yoqne'am, which may suggest that a greater percentage of meat was consumed there, in the main urban center. Interestingly, a sharp change takes place at Tel Yoqne'am later in the Iron Age, with fewer immature animals being slaughtered. Again this could suggest a shift toward wool production or the outsourcing of animals to Assyria.[42]

In Galilee and the north animal bones have been examined from Rosh Zayit, Tel Chinnereth, and Tel Dan. These locations are geographically disparate. Rosh Zayit is in the foothills of Lower Galilee above the Akko plain; Tell Chinnereth is at the northern end of the Sea of Galilee; and Tel Dan is at the head of the Jordan Valley. Nevertheless, their faunal collections bear broad similarities. There is a higher level of wild animals than in the south, and cattle contribute substantially to the samples. It has been suggested that the high level of cattle remains at Rosh Zayit stems from the use of the location as a fort. In this case beef must have been imported for consumption by the military garrison.[43]

Evidence exists at Beth-shean in the Jordan Valley of an agricultural economy based around dry farming.[44] Animal utilization in Transjordan is similar to what we find in the highlands of Cisjordan and in the Negev. In the arid regions of the south there are very few cattle, and the bone assemblages are dominated by caprovines. Herding appears to have followed a mixed strategy with meat, wool, and milk being utilized. Wild animals yield a small component of the animal bones. There are also very few pig remains, and at Tell Nimrin pig utilization drops from 4.7 percent in the Middle Bronze Age to less than 1 percent in the Iron Age.[45] Farther north in a moister region, Hesban has a high level of cattle exploitation (22 percent in Iron Age I and 14 percent in Iron Age II), which probably suggests a more intensive plow-based agriculture rather than cattle herding.[46]

Animal Utilization in the Persian Period

The settlement of Palestine during the Persian period continues to be obscure despite recent research. This is true especially for animal husbandry, where very few faunal remains have been published or sample sizes have been very small.[47] The best finds have been on the coastal plain. At Tel Michal and Ashkelon, where there is data for Iron Age II and the Persian period, no major changes in the patterns of animal exploitation seem to have occurred. The high frequency of mature cattle at Tel Michal suggests a community focused on intensive dry farming. Ashkelon continues to exhibit a very low level of cattle husbandry for a coastal site. There is a dramatic increase in the amount of game, which, it has been suggested, may be due to the presence of a Persian garrison.[48] This might also explain a higher than usual level of goats at the site, which may also have provided meat for the garrison. At Tell el-Hesi in the Shephelah, there is a high frequency of caprovines. Although a higher level of cattle might be expected for the Shephelah, the kill-off patterns suggest that many of the animals were consumed. Unfortunately it is not currently possible to say anything about consumption patterns across the rest of Palestine during the Persian period.

Meat Consumption: A Summary of the Archaeological Evidence

The evidence from animal remains provides a valuable, if complicated, picture of the role of meat in the diet of the ancient Israelites. It is evident that the type and amount of meat available to the inhabitants of Palestine varied according to location and also over time. In general it seems that animals were kept for their secondary products, such as milk and wool, rather than as sources of meat. Nevertheless, it appears that during Iron Age II animals may have increasingly been raised with the purpose of supplying meat. This period of prosperity corresponds to the flourishing of the Israelite kingdoms. The higher level of meat consumption may have come to an end with the conquest of much of Palestine by the Assyrian empire, especially if, as has been suggested, the Assyrians exploited the animal economy of Palestine for themselves.

The evidence from the three sites in the Jezreel Valley — Tell Qiri, Tel Yoqne'am, and Tel Qashish — shows how animal exploitation could vary within a very short distance. Palestine has a number of different ecological niches, and the patterns of animal utilization would have reflected the distinctive constraints of each environment. Nevertheless, it is possible to make some general observations. Pastoral economies were to be found in the central highlands and in the south and east of Palestine. These areas receive a lower rainfall than the north and are less suitable for the practice of dry farming. Nevertheless, cattle utilization increased slightly during the Iron Age. In the Shephelah and on the coastal plain dry farming was pursued. In the early Iron Age pork was an important meat source for the local inhabitants, but this had almost disappeared by Iron Age II. There also existed an important sheep industry that probably produced wool for trade. The wetter climate in the north and in Galilee allowed dry farming to be pursued. Significant tracts of forested land still existed in the Iron Age. Inhabitants of northern towns and villages might still have enjoyed an occasional meal of game, something the inhabitants in the south of Palestine would never have known.

CHAPTER 11

The Consumption of Meat: Anthropological Evidence

Unfortunately the archaeological evidence for meat consumption cannot provide us with quantitative data for how much meat was consumed by individual Israelites. This is, of course, an important issue when considering the Israelite diet and its healthiness. To reflect upon this issue adequately we will need to turn to other sources of information. We have already seen that one possible approach is the combination of archaeological evidence with statistical modeling. Although the results are valuable, a number of assumptions are made that are not easy to sustain. Many Old Testament scholars, as we will see, have relied on anthropological parallels alongside a careful reading of the biblical text. In considering the complex question of meat consumption, it is necessary to take into account all sources of information and the type of contribution they can make to the discussion. We should not decide a priori in favor of one source.

The consensus in Old Testament scholarship that the Israelites rarely consumed meat was established at the end of the nineteenth century with the work of Julius Wellhausen and William Robertson Smith. Wellhausen, for example, argued that "The life of which the blood was regarded as the substance had for the ancient Semites something mysterious and divine about it; they felt a certain religious scruple about destroying it. With them flesh was an uncommon luxury, and they ate it with quite different feelings from those with which they partook of fruits or of milk."[1] This judgment was probably taken from Robertson Smith's important work *The Religion of the Semites*.[2] Smith's views, however, were slightly more nuanced. Smith had observed the occasional nature of meat in the nomadic diet. "Animal food — or at least the flesh of domestic animals, which are the only class of victims admitted among the Semites as ordinary and regular sacrifices — was not a common article of diet even among the nomad Arabs. The everyday food of the nomad consisted of milk, or game, when he could get it, and to a limited extent of dates and meal. . . . Flesh of domestic animals was eaten only as a luxury or in times of famine."[3] Nomadism was, in Smith's time, taken to be the original social form of the Israelite tribes and their patriarchal ancestors. At this point Smith was strongly influenced by the existence of Bedouin in nineteenth-century Palestine, and he believed that their lifestyle was very similar to that of the early Israelites.[4] Nevertheless, later Israelite society had developed beyond nomadism, and Smith held that, in later Israel, flesh was consumed on feast days and holidays.[5] Over time these sacrifices began to be multiplied on trivial occasions, and animal flesh became "a familiar luxury."[6] The influence of the polemic of prophets like Amos is apparent in Smith's account at this point. Smith's nuanced picture of meat consumption in Israel, though written before the archaeological evidence we have examined had surfaced, can find some confirmation in that evidence. In particular the distinction he makes between meat consumption habits in early Israel and in later monarchic Israel fits well with the archaeological picture as we have presented it. Despite the careful distinctions in Smith's view about meat consumption, it was the view that meat was rare that became one of the most influential characterizations of the Israelite diet for subsequent scholarship.

Although parts of Smith's understanding correspond to some of the archaeological evidence, some aspects of his portrayal need modification in light of more recent scholarship. In particular, the theory that the early Israelites were a wave of nomadic tribes from the Arabian Desert has been shown to be mistaken. Early Israelite pastoralists were probably transhumant seminomads, that is, they moved their livestock to different grazing lands according to the season. Nor did the Israelite pastoralists live a nomadic lifestyle removed from settled peoples. Instead, in Palestinian society sedentary and seminomadic elements lived alongside and traded with one another.

We have also seen that selective culling ensures a supply of meat, even where herding strategies emphasize herd security or secondary products. Smith's arguments on this need to be modified in light of the models put forward by Dar, Rosen, and Sasson. Meat consumption in early Israel may have been more frequent than Smith believed. Nevertheless, the models of Dar, Rosen, and Sasson need to take into account the possibility that animal flesh was traded out of the community. This possibility is apparent in recent anthropological work on Palestinian Bedouin. The research of Abu-Rabia, for example, shows that modern Palestinian Bedouin are not a self-contained nomadic society, but interact and trade with sedentary populations. Over a year's time, the Bedouin families examined by Abu-Rabia frequently sold animals in order to purchase goods not produced by the family. In fact, the majority of the animals were sold. More interesting is Abu-Rabia's finding that a family with a more nomadic existence slaughtered fewer of its animals for self-consumption than a family with a more sedentary existence.[7] The social, political, and economic differences between modern Bedouin society and ancient Israelite seminomadism need to be carefully weighed. Even taking this into account, such results again appear to confirm Robertson Smith's account of the changing patterns of meat consumption in ancient Israel.

Smith's chronological account also needs to be modified. We can agree with him that as Israel developed and became a state with greater centralization and urbanization, more Israelites became sedentary than in earlier periods. As such the population as a whole may have consumed more meat. Nevertheless, we do not have a transition from nomadism to sedentariness at one point in time; rather we have a complex society in which various options existed along a spectrum from nomadism to settledness. As Israel developed over time; the boundaries between different groups and the strategies they pursued changed. Thus, even later in Iron Age II some groups would have pursued a seminomadic pastoralism, traded with their sedentary neighbors, and enjoyed less meat in their diet.

The picture of meat consumption in Israel will therefore have to be more complex than has usually been suggested. It is not the case that Israelites "ate meat only rarely," but it is equally misleading to suggest that meat appeared regularly on their tables. Habits of meat consumption changed over time and according to sociopolitical realities. The consumption of meat in premonarchic times was probably a relatively infrequent event, but it became more common during the Israelite monarchies — at least in certain circles. The absorption of the kingdom of Israel into the Assyrian empire, and Judah's acceptance of vassal status, may well have resulted in meat consumption dropping in Judean and former Israelite areas.

There remains, however, another aspect to the problem of the level of meat consumption that we have not yet covered. The question of meat consumption raises a problem we saw in the previous chapter, that of distribution. Even if we know that animals needed to be culled and that meat was available to a community, how much was consumed within that community and how much was traded outside it? Within the community, did all receive an equal share or did some have greater claim? To answer these questions, we will now turn to the issues of production and distribution.

CHAPTER 12

Food Distribution

The second of the five stages in the food process that Jack Goody identifies is distribution.[1] When we think of the ancient Israelite diet, this stage is extremely important but often overlooked. This is apparent in the models constructed by Dar, Rosen, and Sasson. Calculating the amount of food available per capita is appropriate only if we can show that it is distributed in an equitable manner. This is proved by food crises in the present day, where it is often said that there is enough food to feed the earth's population if only it were distributed evenly. The reality of our modern world is that this is not the case, and while food goes to waste in the West, people starve in sub-Saharan Africa. The question is, what was the situation in ancient Palestine?

The sites to which Rosen and Sasson give particular attention date from the early Iron Age, that is, the premonarchic period in Israel. This is not without reason. Immediately prior to this period the great empires of the Late Bronze Age collapsed and no major political powers had formed to fill the power vacuum. Social and political structures were thus found mainly at the regional or town level, and international trade diminished considerably compared to the Late Bronze Age. As a result this period in Israel's history — which in biblical terms is described as the tribal period or the time of the judges — is often believed to have little in the way of social hierarchies; communities were self-supporting. Consequently, this period saw, according to some biblical scholars, the development of an ideology of egalitarianism. All Israelites enjoyed the same status before Israel's God. This ideology was developed in response to the strong hierarchical structure of Canaanite society, and was later to result in an ambivalence toward the institution of kingship during the time of Samuel.[2] With this operating ideology of egalitarianism within Israel, it would appear that the assumptions of Dar, Rosen, and Sasson about a relatively equitable distribution of food are reasonable.

More recent scholarship has questioned whether this in fact represents a romantic reading of the premonarchic period that not only reads later ideals back into an earlier time but also fails to take into account evidence that counters it. Some recent models of early Israelite society argue that although society was more homogenous than in earlier or later periods, socioeconomic differentiation was not absent.[3] Additionally, it has been suggested that even in this period the Israelite villages were not subsistence communities, but that trade took place between neighboring towns and villages.[4] Thus, the basic assumptions that underpin the models of Dar, Rosen, and Sasson must be called into question.

An examination of the biblical texts confirms our suspicions about an equitable distribution of food resources. First, it is well known that Israel was a patriarchal society, and thus, at the level of the family, there was a social hierarchy. The head of the family appears to have had the right to determine how food was distributed among family members (1 Sam. 1:5; cf. Gen. 43:34). It seems likely that prestigious foods, such as meat, would have been distributed with preference given to the family head and his male children.[5] Second, from earliest periods there existed a male, priestly elite. For an animal to be eaten it had to be sacrificed, and this had to take place at the sanctuary with an officiating priest. The priest had a right to some of the sacrificial meat (1 Sam. 2). In other words, the sacrificial system resulted in meat being distributed in a way that favored the priestly elite. Thus, even in the premonarchic period the best food resources were being diverted toward elite males.[6]

When the monarchy was established, these patterns of redistribution occurred on a national scale. One of the striking features of Solomon's reign, according to 1 Kings, is a sumptuous royal table. Twelve district officials were responsible for supplying the king's table, each for a month of the year. According to 1 Kings 4:22-23, the table's daily supply was substantial: "thirty cors of fine flour and sixty cors of meal, ten fattened cattle, twenty pastured cattle, and a hundred sheep, besides deer, gazelles, roebucks and fatted fowl." That ordinary Israelite farmers would lose some of their agricultural income had already been anticipated by the prophet

Samuel according to 1 Samuel 8:15: "the king will require a tenth of your seed and your vineyards, and he will give it to his officials and servants." Thus, Solomon's table fed the new royal elite, but did so by redistributing food from elsewhere in Israel.

According to the biblical account, the heavy burden of Solomon's court was the principal reason the united monarchy divided into two separate kingdoms. If so, it is still likely that redistribution continued, if on a less impressive scale. The Israelite kingdoms became societies that were increasingly more differentiated socially. A relatively small elite enjoyed a proportionately larger share of the food resources, especially those that were more prestigious. Certainly Amos appears to have such an elite in mind when he releases some of his invective:

> Those who lie on beds of ivory,
> And lounge on their couches,
> Who eat lamb from the flocks
> And calves from the midst of the stalls,
> Who strum upon the harp
> Like David composing songs for themselves
>   on musical instruments,
> Who drink wine from bowls
> And anoint themselves with oils.
>
> (6:4-6; cf. 4:1; Isa. 5:11-12).[7]

The incorporation of Israel into the Assyrian empire and Judah's status as an Assyrian vassal brought to bear a new sociopolitical reality with potential implications for food supply and distribution. We have already seen that animal remains from the Assyrian period suggest that animals may have been exported to Assyria for consumption. Thus, the new imperial reality brought a dimension to redistribution that had not previously been experienced within the Israelite kingdoms. In addition, in later periods imperial military garrisons consumed a higher level of game and beef. The reduced supply of meat would have affected local elites, who would have seen their access to meat severely reduced, and nonelites, who may have lost access to meat almost entirely.

CHAPTER 13

Nutritional Deficiencies

The possibility that ancient diets, dominated by cereal consumption, might give rise to nutritional deficiencies was first raised by Rosemary Ellison in a discussion of Mesopotamian diet.[1] Considering the possibility that the diet of workers who received barley rations was not supplemented with any other food, she concluded that for such a diet "the most obvious nutritional deficiencies in the barley rations were those of vitamin C and vitamin A."[2] Good sources of vitamin A are dairy products, animal livers, and the green leaves of plants; vitamin C is found in fruits and vegetables as well as fresh meat. In the ancient Near East, where diets may well have been low in animal foods, fruits, and vegetables, serious deficiencies could occur. Vitamin A deficiency is associated with a variety of eye diseases, including night blindness, xerophthalmia, and blindness.[3] Vitamin C deficiency may lead to scurvy, though occurrences of scurvy may well have been seasonal.[4]

As Peter Garnsey notes in his study of Roman diets, another possible nutritional deficiency in diets with a high cereal content is iron deficiency anemia. Bran has a very high content of phytate, which inhibits iron absorption.[5] In ancient Israel cereals were probably frequently consumed as chapatis made from flour with a high extraction rate (undersieved), and thus the bran and phytate intake of ancient Israelites would have been high. Consequently iron deficiency anemia may have been common, particularly among children and pregnant women. Iron deficiency affects brain function and the immune system, and can reduce working capacity. Even in the present, it is the most common nutritional deficiency disorder, and is particularly prevalent in nonindustrialized countries.[6] Zinc deficiency has also been linked to diets with a high intake of phytate and a low intake of animal proteins. The human body has a sophisticated mechanism for controlling zinc absorption such that when zinc levels are low the stomach absorbs higher levels of zinc if digesting foods with a zinc content. Nevertheless, in a very narrow diet almost entirely based on unleavened wholemeal bread, growth retardation and delayed sexual maturation may result in children. Cases of zinc deficiency have been known in the modern Middle East, for example, in Egypt and Iran.[7]

One might think the large agricultural majority in Israel would have enjoyed a better nutritional status than the small number who pursued pastoralism. The reverse was probably the case. A diet focused on milk-based products is high in protein, and supplementation with cereals makes up the deficiency in energy provision. The pastoralist diet, with its diversity, is usually understood to be healthier than a cereal-based diet.[8] Vitamin A deficiency would probably have been less prevalent, though the diet probably lacked sufficient access to vitamin C and iron. In cases of drought, however, flocks would have provided a means of food storage for only a limited time, and pastoralists were thus more vulnerable to famine conditions than their sedentary neighbors. In other words, Israelite pastoralists who settled down and pursued a sedentary existence based on agriculture exchanged a better diet for greater food security.

Critical reconstruction of Israelite diets and comparison with contemporary preindustrialized diets provide some basis for suspecting that the nutritional status of ancient Israel's population may have fallen short of ideal. A degree of substantiation can be provided by paleopathological research. Paleopathology is the scientific study of human skeletal remains. Modern advances in paleopathology mean that skeletal remains can provide evidence of a limited number of nutritional diseases and deficiencies. These include "vitamin D deficiency, vitamin C deficiency, iodine deficiency, iron deficiency, excessive dietary fluorine, protein-calorie deficiency, and trace element deficiencies."[9] In addition, teeth can give some indication of diet, and other features may point to the health of a population, such as age at death and stature.

Unfortunately the potential of paleopathology to contribute to our examination of the Israelite diet is restricted by the paucity of studies on skeletal remains from Iron Age or Persian period Israel. One reason for this is that relatively few Iron Age burial sites (particularly Iron Age I) have been discovered in the central Israelite areas.[10] Yet even when they have been found, other factors have conspired against their utilization for paleopathological research. During much of the twentieth century archaeology, particularly in its manifestation as "biblical archaeology," had little use for human remains. Archaeological research focused almost exclusively on pottery, buildings, inscriptions, and other material remains.[11] Second, when remains were discovered, many of the indicators of nutritional stress that are now recognized had not been identified.[12] There are also the religious and ethical sensibilities of orthodox Jews, many of whom object to Jewish remains being disturbed. In recent times the growing political strength of orthodox groups has severely restricted the paleopathological work undertaken on human remains discovered accidentally or during excavations. Since the paleopathological examination of skeletal material from Iron Age Israel has been so limited, critical use will be made of studies from neighboring areas in the southern Levant or from proximate periods.

Where paleopathological investigation has been conducted, careful attention must be given to the nature of the finds. The number of individual remains discovered at a site tends to be relatively small, making statistical analysis precarious. In addition, remains may not be well preserved. The ideal situation is to find complete skeletons that are clearly distinct from other skeletal remains. Unfortunately, burial sites from ancient Palestine usually contain the skeletal remains of many individuals. In addition, skeletal remains were often subjected to secondary burial, in which, after a body decomposed, the bones were collected and placed with the skeletal remains of others, often at the back of the tomb. Thus, skeletal remains are often mixed and fragmentary. Finally, for various reasons paleopathologists may have applied only certain forms of analysis.[13]

For Iron Age Israel the most important study undertaken was upon the skeletal remains of sixty individuals found in Jerusalem and dated to the seventh century B.C.[14] This group included seventeen examples of a condition known as cribra orbitalia (31.5 percent). Cribra orbitalia and the closely related porotic hyperostosis are pathologies of the cranium that have often been discussed as possible indicators of iron deficiency. Both terms are used to describe lesions on different parts of the skull. In skeletal remains, "these lesions are characterized by pitting of the compact bone, usually associated with an increase in the thickness of the adjacent diploic bone. The lesions can vary in size from less than 1mm in diameter to large, coalescing apertures, and are found on the orbital roof and skull vault, particularly the frontal, parietal, and occipital bones."[15] The condition occurs in childhood and results from iron-deficiency anemia: a reduction below normal in the concentration of hemoglobin or red blood cells.[16] This condition has been commonly associated with an inadequate diet, though caution must be exercised here, for iron-deficiency anemia has a number of possible causes. In particular, iron deficiency may be part of the body's defense against infection, and consequently better judged as evidence of a high exposure to infectious diseases.[17] It may not be necessary to choose between inadequate diet and high exposure to infection, however. Vulnerability to disease and poor nutritional status have a symbiotic relationship. Thus evidence of chronic iron-deficiency may still provide indirect evidence of poor nutrition.[18] The occurrence of cribra orbitalia in the Iron Age population of Jerusalem is in no way unusual for historical Palestine. We find similar levels in other historical periods.[19]

The individuals from Jerusalem also exhibited dental pathologies, including tooth decay (16 percent), predeath tooth loss (50 percent), and alveolar abscesses (16 percent).[20] The level of carious teeth or tooth decay is comparable to a small collection of twenty skulls from Lachish, where four of the skulls had evidence of caries.[21] It is below that of the Roman and Byzantine periods, but is part of a steady upward trend visible in the southern Levant from the Neolithic period.[22] Tooth decay is associated with a diet high in cooked carbohydrates.[23] Tooth loss and alveolar abscesses are indicators of gum disease resulting from the accumulation of plaque. The soft sticky foods, such as gruels and porridges, that have characterized human diet since the beginnings of agriculture are often noted as the likely cause of these pathologies in premodern populations.

Evidence of predeath tooth loss has also been found in the sixty-five skeletal remains from Iron Age Tell 'Ira in the Beersheba Valley. Poor preservation meant that a full study of dental pathology was impossible, though the excavators also noted evidence of severe attrition on the few maxillae that were found.[24] Teeth attrition is a common finding across communities practicing agriculture in the ancient Near East and results from an abrasive diet. The process of making bread included grinding grain with a stone quern. This tended to introduce sand and pieces of grit into the flour used for baking bread.

Important skeletal remains have also been discovered at Tell el-Mazar, Achzib, and Tel Michal. These locations lie on the border of historical Israelite territory, or even in what was non-Israelite territory. Though none of the sites are in central Israelite territory, they provide useful evidence of the health and nutrition of neighboring peoples. We have no grounds for thinking that the diet of these people varied considerably from that of the Israelites. Tell el-Mazar is located 3 kilometers east of the river Jordan, half-way down the Jordan Valley, close to Tell Deir 'Alla. The skeletal remains date from late Iron Age II and the Persian period. Achzib lies on the coastal plain north of Akko. Although assigned to the tribe of Asher in Joshua 19, it lies within Phoenician territory, and the material remains from the exca-vated tombs are characteristically Phoenician. The skeletal remains date from the ninth to the sixth centuries B.C. Tel Michal is also located on the coastal plain a few kilometers north of the mouth of the Yarkon River. The skeletal remains came from a Persian period cemetery.

The skeletal remains from Tell el-Mazar have been examined for den-tal pathologies. Unfortunately they have not been given a full statistical analysis. The teeth show evidence of various dental pathologies, including a condition known as enamel hypoplasia. The occurrence of hypoplasia is a further important indicator of poor health and nutrition. It is a condi-tion that "results in defects on the enamel of the teeth in the form of pits or grooves."[25] This occurs during childhood when enamel formation is arrested due to environmental stress from disease or malnutrition. "[E]namel is formed according to a strict chronological sequence and once formed, undergoes no repair or regeneration. The location and severity of developmental defects in the enamel then provide a permanent record of the severity of environmental stress during the period of enamel forma-tion."[26] Additionally, remains from three infants signaled a significant dis-crepancy between the skeletal age and the dental age. The anthropologists examining the bones suggested that this is possibly evidence of malnutri-tion.[27]

At Achzib fifty fragmentary skeletal remains were discovered. The teeth that had survived exhibited a 45 percent incidence of enamel hypoplasia.[28] When compared to other Levantine populations from differ-ent periods, this level of enamel hypoplasia is not unusual. Indeed, if any-thing, it occurred slightly less frequently at Achzib. Bronze Age popula-tions at Jericho and Jebel Qa'aqir were around 50 to 60 percent, and at Sasa in Upper Galilee were over 90 percent. For Roman Jerusalem and Ein Gedi 50 percent of individuals exhibited hypoplasia.[29]

At Tel Michal the remains of twenty-six adults were discovered. These remains were examined not for physical signs of nutritional deficiencies, but for the presence of certain trace elements in the bones that could indicate dietary habits. Three elements are particularly important for our interest in diet: strontium, calcium, and zinc. We have already noted the importance of zinc in human diet. The ratio of strontium and calcium can be an important indicator of diet due to the different manner in which plants and mammals absorb these elements. In plants no discrimination is made between strontium and calcium, and the ratio of the two is identical to that of the water and soil of the local area. Mammals, on the other hand, absorb more calcium than strontium in the digestive process, and their bones exhibit a lower strontium-calcium ratio. The higher up the food chain, the lower the strontium-calcium ratio; herbivores have the highest ratio while carnivores have the lowest. Consequently, a comparison of the strontium-calcium ratio of human bones with that of the bones of herbivores can suggest the level of meat consumption.[30]

The calcium-strontium ratio of the human population from Tel Michal was compared to the results obtained from ancient populations in Greece. Tel Michal had the lowest ratio, suggesting that the population consumed relatively large amounts of animal meat and obtained a smaller amount of their protein requirements from plants. On the other hand, the level of zinc was low compared to the ancient Greek populations. This is surprising, since the best source for zinc is red meat. The most obvious cause of this low level of zinc is that zinc absorption is inhibited by a diet high in phytates. Sara Bisel, the anthropologist who worked on the Tel Michal remains, concludes that "the Tel Michal people of the Persian period ate unleavened flatbread and unrefined cereals."[31] If correct, this would be an interesting conclusion. It would provide some confirmation for our arguments that we must reckon with a higher level of meat consumption in ancient Israel than was traditionally granted. On the other hand, it would undermine any easy assumption that a diet slightly richer in meat than other ancient diets is necessarily healthier.

Paleopathology makes an important contribution to our understanding of the diet of the Iron Age population in the south Levant. Since skeletal remains from very few sites have been examined, results from individual locations must be treated with care. However, the evidence for nutritional deficiencies is consistent with pathological trends for other periods in Palestinian history, and it is within this broader context that the evidence should be considered. Iron Age Israel was no different from earlier and later periods in exhibiting a high level of pathologies that relate to poor nutritional status and acute infection. Seventh century B.C. Jerusalem had high levels of iron-deficiency anemia, and earlier and later populations of Palestine suffered similarly high levels of anemia. As we observed, the level of enamel hypoplasia at Achzib is slightly lower than at other sites from earlier and later periods. Future discoveries may show whether this is a singularity or not. For other periods levels of hypoplasia are above 50 percent, and it is possible that Achzib's location on the coastal plain afforded its inhabitants a better diet than was enjoyed elsewhere. Whether this is the case or not, Achzib had only a slightly better occurrence of hypoplasia, at a level still high enough for us to conclude that the health of the population was far from good.

We have already noted that poor diet and susceptibility to disease are symbiotic. It follows, therefore, that populations with poor diet are likely to have a lower life expectancy. Human mortality may of course result from numerous causes, but high levels of mortality are an important indicator of environmental stress. Only in very rare cases will lack of nutrition lead directly to death, but poor nutrition increases vulnerability to disease. Mortality profiles are therefore a good indicator of the health status of a population, for which nutrition plays a significant role. Life expectancy in all ancient populations was poor, but the evidence shows that life expectancy at Iron Age sites was markedly lower than in the preceding Bronze Age or the Hellenistic and Roman periods that followed.[32] Despite the fragmentary nature of the remains at Tell 'Ira, it was possible to produce a mortality profile. The demography of Tell 'Ira remains shows high mortality during early childhood, adolescence, and around age 35 to 45, with the average life span of the adult population only 36.9 years. Since there are no signs of violence and the observed pathologies are primarily degenerative, the excavators conclude that "this population lived a peaceful and healthy life being probably engaged in intensive agriculture."[33] It seems safe to assume a peaceful existence, but the claims for healthiness seem less well grounded, especially when compared to other periods. This does appear to be part of a pattern for the Iron Age and Persian period, since the populations at Tell el-Mazar, Achzib, and Tel Michal show similarly poor profiles.[34]

Only further discoveries will confirm whether or not the small number of results we have are representative of the demography in ancient Israel, but currently the evidence suggests that the population of ancient Israel did not enjoy good health. These demographic patterns are consistent with those from many other premodern agricultural communities. They suggest that most people had a short life, with a high level of infant mortality and few adults surviving beyond the age of fifty. This cannot be attributed to nutrition alone, but there are good grounds for thinking that poor nutrition played a contributory role.

Finally, the height of human skeletal remains may point to levels of nutrition. In his study of the Persian period skeletal remains from Tell Qiri, a site in the Jezreel Valley, Baruch Arensberg observes that "Females appear to have been rather short, averaging 152cm, whereas males tend to have been tall (171cm). The mean difference in stature between the sexes (c. 19cm) is greater than in present-day populations (mean 12cm), suggesting some unfavourable social conditions discriminating against the women at the time, perhaps in food consumption."[35] Arensberg's sample is extremely small, consisting of only five males and three females, and must be regarded as a vulnerable result on statistical grounds. Nevertheless, a similar discrepancy for a much larger sample was observed in Hellenistic and early Roman skeletal remains from Samaria and the Shephelah.[36] Further study with more samples will be needed if Arensberg's suggestion is to be substantiated. Should they be discovered to be representative, they would support our arguments that the distribution of meat, and possibly other foods, favored men over women.

The study of human skeletal remains from Israel and their pathologies confirms a number of the arguments made in previous chapters about the healthiness of the Israelite diet. The discovery of new remains and new techniques increases the hope that our knowledge will be further augmented in the future. Our current state of knowledge suggests that the population of Iron Age Israel generally suffered from an inadequate diet, poor health, and low life expectancy. Their experience was little different from that of other premodern inhabitants of Palestine, and in some respects it may even have been worse.

CONCLUSION

Our examination of the various issues and evidence that must be considered in reconstructing the Israelite diet allows us to provide a critical account of the ancient Israelite diet, its variety and its healthiness (chapter 14). This account of the Israelite diet allows us to reflect on the claims made by "biblical diets" and to consider briefly what the Old Testament might have to say about eating and drinking today (chapter 15).

The Diet of the Ancient Israelites

What food did the ancient Israelites eat? This deceptively simply question confronts us with a complex topic that must include insights from biblical interpretation, recent archaeological work — including the specialized disciplines of paleopathology and zooarchaeology — geography, and social anthropology. The diverse areas of knowledge that must be taken into account are a challenge to the individual scholar, not only because research expertise is narrowly focused, but also because these areas of knowledge must be adequately integrated. With this challenge, though, comes opportunity to think clearly about how separate intellectual disciplines might relate to one another around a common topic. The problem with many considerations of diet, in my view, is that they fail to acknowledge the diverse evidence that must be considered and thus provide an inaccurate picture. Unfortunately the limitations of our knowledge mean that we will only ever have a partial glimpse into the Israelite diet. We have a complex Sudoku puzzle but not enough numbers to solve the puzzle. Nevertheless, we might hope to make some progress and fill in some other numbers. What we cannot do is rely on a single approach, for this will get us only so far. Any serious attempt to solve this puzzle will have to operate on numerous levels, as indeed we have attempted to do.

In terms of generalities we can at least say that textual and archaeological evidence agree in the centrality of the so-called Mediterranean triad: bread, wine, and olive oil. Fruit, vegetables, legumes, milk products, and meat made a much smaller contribution to caloric intake. There are good grounds for suspecting that this diet was nutritionally unsatisfactory, even where sufficient calories were consumed. Probable deficiencies were vitamin A, vitamin C, and iron. At lower social levels the diet was probably more monotonous and vulnerable. The level of meat consumption has often been a subject of disagreement. Since animal husbandry involves some level of culling, that is, not all animals are kept until maturity, and since most animals were kept within the Syro-Palestinian economy (at least before the Assyrian expansion), we must assume a higher level of meat consumption than was assumed by earlier scholarship. However, we must reckon with the possibility that distribution was uneven.

Such observations about food distribution in Israel point to the difficulties with the language of a singular Israelite *diet*. We should not speak of Israelite diets, which would suggest a greater diversity than is merited, but we must recognize the existence of considerable diversity within the Israelite diet. We can identify at least three interrelated axes that produced dietary variation in ancient Israel: geographical, temporal, and social.

First, there is geographical variation. The numerous ecological niches in ancient Israel resulted in varying subsistence strategies, not least along a spectrum between seminomadic pastoralism and settled mixed agriculture. Cereals were the most important dietary component for pastoralists as well as their sedentary neighbors, but the pastoralist diet would have had a higher level of milk products. Depending on the region, the diet of Israelite villagers could have included legumes, vegetables, and fruit. Certain towns and districts would have been close to trading routes, and some parts of the population would have benefited from a greater variety of foods resulting from trade. We know, for example, that fish was consumed to a greater extent than previously imagined. Yet it is likely that imported fish was readily available only in some of the larger cities in Israel.

Second, there were temporal variations. This was true on an annual basis. Some fruits and vegetables have limited storage possibilities; fresh milk would have been available for only some of the year; meat consumption occurred at particular moments determined by a calendar that marked important seasonal and religious occasions. There were also changes during Israel's history, not so much due to new foods (although the chicken was introduced at some point in the first millennium B.C.), but to individual diets resulting from expanding trade or changing social structure. We have seen how meat consumption changed over time as Israel moved from being a collection of disparate tribal groups through being independent kingdoms to being incorporated into the Mesopotamian empires.

Third, dietary variation occurred along social lines. This is especially the case with traded foodstuffs, such as fish, and prestige foods, such as meat or fruit. The elite diet was probably more varied and had certain foods that were not available to poorer Israelites. The differences between elite and ordinary Israelites would have been particularly pronounced during the periodic famines that occurred in Palestine, when access to basic foodstuffs became difficult. There may also have been variation within smaller social units, such as the family. Certain foods were considered more prestigious, and it is likely that husbands and sons consumed a greater proportion of meat and other foods than wives and daughters.

CHAPTER 15

Biblical Diets

In the last forty years there has been an increasing interest in "biblical diets," especially among evangelical Protestants in North America.[1] Whether as a means of slimming or out of a desire to eat better, there appears to be an insatiable appetite for books that offer dietary advice on the basis of biblical interpretation. Clearly this reflects widely shared concerns about American health and increased body consciousness in an image-dominated age, but "biblical diets" place such concerns within a religious and theological framework. It would not be possible to analyze all the attempts to offer dietary advice on the basis of the Bible, and so in this chapter we will consider a small sample of recent attempts: Don Colbert's *What Would Jesus Eat?*, Joyce Rogers's *The Bible's Seven Secrets to Healthy Eating*, Jordan Rubin's *The Maker's Diet*, and Rex Russell's *What the Bible Says about Healthy Living*.[2] We will examine some of the claims made about such "biblical diets," and consider some of the weaknesses of these books, before offering brief reflections about what the Old Testament has to say about food that may be of relevance at the beginning of the twenty-first century.

As well as advocating its own distinctive "biblical diet" — sometimes in controversy with other purported "biblical diets" — each of these four books has its own subordinate concerns. Don Colbert is especially exercised over the amount of processed, sugary foods Americans eat, and his call to eat as Jesus would have eaten is an appeal for whole-grain breads, pure water, and fresh fruits and vegetables. Joyce Rogers, a homemaker, has similar concerns, but also combines dietary advice with spiritual counsel.

Each chapter of her book not only advocates a food found in the Bible, but also explores its use as a spiritual metaphor. Rex Russell, a radiologist, is negative about corporate America and frequently uses discussion of diet to springboard into antievolution polemic. A strong creationist bent is presumably what lies behind Russell's advice that dinosaur eggs be avoided![3] Jordan Rubin holds a romanticized view of the health and diet of primitive peoples. This entails a strong rejection of most aspects of conventional health care, including vaccinations, medication, and doctors.[4] Ironically *The Maker's Diet* includes the usual disclaimer that the reader consult with her own physician about any dietary changes.

It is important to the self-presentation of these books that the Bible is seen as the primary source for dietary information with modern nutritional science playing a subordinate role.[5] The books typically indulge in the language of other popular dietary books as well as creating their own novel categories. Thus, processed foods provide "empty calories" and are "dead" or "sterile," food is divided into "good" and "bad," nonkosher meat is "toxic." The Bible is also thought to operate with similar categories. Thus, for example, it is considered possible to give a biblical definition of "milk" and measure modern pasteurized milk against it. The complexities of human nutrition and the existence of scholarly disagreement can be exploited disingenuously. Opposing arguments are not considered on their merits but are juxtaposed to cancel each other out. Scientific evidence can be used to justify the biblical diet or presented as an incoherent cacophony such that the "biblical" view can be presented as final arbiter. The result is biblical proof texting and unverified statements: "I think," "I believe," even "I predict."

The writers of the dietary books appeal to their readers not only by promising a healthier body, but also by appealing to the altruism of evangelism. If a biblical diet is followed correctly, the inevitable result will be a glowing health, freedom from illness, and an excellent figure. As a result, nonbelievers will inquire after the believer's health and so be led to the Bible and to Christ. Dieting is, consequently, a spiritual exercise, a bodily equivalent of the evangelical quiet time. Through changes to one's private life — what one eats in the privacy of one's home — changes to one's public persona will result. Dieting as spiritual exercise requires daily discipline and self-control, and like the quiet time, is vulnerable to feelings of guilt, self-loathing, and personal failure.

As health and dietary advice, the books run from the helpful through to the potentially dangerous. With its emphasis on whole-grain bread, fresh fruits and vegetables, exercise, fish and only occasional meat, and its warnings about processed and fast foods, Colbert's *What Would Jesus Eat?* is good advice, albeit for the wrong reasons. On the other hand, as we will see, Rubin's *The Maker's Diet* subscribes to an unconventional nutritional viewpoint that is skeptical about the dangers of cholesterol and saturated fat. Combined with its testimonies of healing from cancer and other serious illnesses,[6] and its skepticism toward modern medical care, it is potentially harmful. My primary concern, though, is not to examine the dietary soundness of the biblical diets, but their biblical interpretation.

Biblical Interpretation

It is relatively simple to find examples of mistaken biblical interpretation. It is with a delicious irony that Russell writes, "In the seventh century [eighth century!] before Christ, Hosea, the prophet to the kingdom of Judah [Israel!], uttered this doleful lament: 'My people are destroyed from lack of knowledge (Hos. 4.6).'"[7] Reliance upon the Authorized Version (AV) increases the possibility of interpretative errors. Russell finds herbs in Genesis 1:11-12, and Rubin mistakenly understands Isaiah 7:15 to be implying the influence of butter and honey on brain function. It is easy to see how the AV's "curds and honey He shall eat, that He may know to refuse the evil and choose the good" could be misunderstood in this way.[8] Colbert is given to questionable assumptions that go beyond the biblical text. According to him, the Israelites fished in the Red Sea after their departure from Egypt, and elsewhere he assures his readers that cheese was often mixed with garlic, parsley, thyme, or dill in biblical times.[9] Some assumptions are indebted to the arguments of creationists. The extraordinary life spans of the people before the flood are attributed to their vegetarian diets.[10]

All the books share a belief that the dietary laws in Leviticus 11 and Deuteronomy 14 still have value as dietary instructions for Christians. Although this is a departure from traditional Christian thought and some New Testament texts, the dietary laws are important to the authors of "biblical diets" because they appear to justify the view of the Bible as a nutritional handbook. In this view the dietary laws were given to the Israelites because certain meat products were unhealthy or potentially poisonous.

Biblical scholars long ago abandoned such ideas and sought to understand the dietary laws within the social and symbolic context of Leviticus.[11] Through an American Protestant lens, however, these cannot be laws that have to be obeyed, merely the Creator's advice that we would do well to heed.[12] The dietary laws are often read in conjunction with Exodus 15:26: "If you will listen carefully to the voice of YHWH your God, and do what is right in his sight, and give heed to his commandments and keep all his statutes, I will not bring upon you all the diseases that I brought upon the Egyptians," which with its reference to freedom from disease is a favorite proof text of biblical diet advocates. The reference to the plagues in Exodus is missed and understood instead as natural illness resulting from the poor diet of the Egyptians. In addition, the context of God's covenantal relationship with his people is completely elided and the verse becomes a mechanistic promise valid for anyone who follows the dietary laws whatever their creed.

The "would" of Colbert's *What Would Jesus Eat?* clearly allows considerable latitude, especially since the New Testament gives us little insight into what Jesus ate. On the one hand, reasonable inferences can be made about Jesus' diet. Bread, fish, and vegetables probably were significant elements of his diet, and it is unlikely that he ate nonkosher meat. On the other hand, it is a leap of imagination to assert that Jesus "ate eggs and clean poultry . . . stripped of excess fat and eaten sparingly."[13] It may be convenient to hold this view if Jesus is to be a model for modern nutrition, but it can be little more than assertion. The same is true of the claim that "Jesus ate a balanced diet."[14] As we have seen, the ancient Israelite diet was not balanced, and this probably did not change in the Greco-Roman period.

"Would" also means that Colbert can draw conclusions about foodstuffs unknown in Roman Palestine. This includes fruits and vegetables that were not introduced into the Mediterranean world until a later period. "Unfortunately, soybeans were not available in Israel at the time of Jesus. Had they been, I feel certain that Jesus would have eaten them regularly."[15] On the other hand, Colbert is also firmly convinced that Jesus would have eschewed all forms of processed and fast foods. The tension between what Jesus did eat, what he would have eaten, and what he ought to have eaten is particularly clear in the discussion of wine. Colbert knows that the biblical references to wine cannot be explained away as nonalcoholic grape juice, and the health benefits of red wine in moderation have been widely publicized. Yet this would be a difficult argument for teetotal Christians to swallow, and so, while Colbert allows the drinking of wine, "I strongly encourage my patients as well as my readers to choose a non-alcoholic red wine substitute, red wine capsules, or a supplement that contains the powerful phytonutrients quercetin and resveratrol."[16] The same problem confronts Rogers, though she does not admit it. Instead, she moves seamlessly from wine to grape juice, a fact to which her index bears witness, since only grape juice figures in it.[17]

It is clear from Colbert's and Rogers's discussion of wine that, despite claims to the contrary, the agenda for the "biblical diets" is frequently driven by considerations other than exegesis of the Bible. This is true of the diets as a whole. The reconstructed biblical diet proves prophetically nutritious and remarkably congruent with current dietary advice. The realities of the Israelite diet were, as we have seen, far from the nutritional ideal, and skeletal evidence points to their poor health and life expectancy. This despite Rubin's claim that the Israelites were "the healthiest people in the world."[18]

It is Rubin's *Maker's Diet* that is most captive to one particular food philosophy. Rubin's commitments are indicated obtusely in his introductory praise for the work of Weston Price, a dentist who in the 1940s advocated the diets of primitive peoples. Price's unorthodox views on nutrition now find modern advocates in the form of the Weston Price Foundation. Rubin himself is on the honorary board.[19] Rubin's "biblical diet" shares all the dietary emphases of the Foundation: skepticism about the harmful effects of cholesterol and saturated fats, the advocacy of a diet high in meat and milk consumption, a love of sprouting grains and a hatred of soy products. All these emphases are justified by Rubin as biblical.

Biblical Food and the Bible on Food

The books on biblical diet are easily shown to contain examples of biblical interpretation that are misinformed, whimsical, confused, and dominated by agendas that are alien to the Bible. Yet such works clearly have a powerful appeal and sell thousands of copies. On the one hand, they are a distinctly Christian reflection of the obsession with body image reflected in American society more generally. Yet they fail to place such obsessions under searching theological critique and accept the values of our modern culture as normative. On the other hand, they also seem to reflect a concern that many Protestant denominations have stressed the soul and the intellect at the expense of the body.[20] These two observations are, to my mind, closely linked. They reflect the lack of serious reflection on the body in some sections of modern Protestantism.

If the appetite for "biblical diets" represents such inadequacies in modern Protestant thinking, it would be unfair and pastorally inappropriate to treat those who read such books with contempt. Hundreds of thousands of well-intentioned Christians are offered diets that many will not be able to keep, for these diets are no different from other dietary practices in this respect. For those who fail to keep to these diets or who do not see their weight dropping as they expect, the result is likely to be guilt, depression, and self-loathing. For those following a "biblical diet," however, this will not only be physical, mental, and emotional, but also spiritual. The failure to keep a "biblical diet" will easily be seen as failing God.

It is hardly possible here to develop a theology of the body, even were I able. Nevertheless, it is surely necessary to say something about food. To do so is to try and grasp how, in an extended discussion about food and what a Christian should eat, the apostle Paul can state that "the kingdom of God is not a matter of eating and drinking, but of righteousness, peace and joy in the Holy Spirit" (Rom. 14:17). In other words, the kingdom is not about eating and drinking, but also paradoxically is! Examined in context, what one eats is clearly not the issue for Paul, but how one eats is. Is it done "as to the Lord," that is, with an eye to one's fellow Christian brother or sister? More broadly, the Bible does have much to say about the body and, indeed, about food. The horizon, however, would do well to move from *biblical food* to the *Bible on food*. The Bible does not purport to offer dietary advice, but it does frequently touch upon food and human responses to it. I offer four examples.[21]

A recurring concern of some of the biblical diets is organic food. This is driven by health concerns, though it could better be related to the concern about land and justice in many Old Testament texts. Only in recent years has biblical scholarship given sustained attention to the theme of land and ecology in the Old Testament; nevertheless, it is an important topic. Leviticus 17–26, for example, envisages the land as a divine possession. The Israelites are merely tenant farmers. The Jubilee laws envisage a regular Sabbath for the land, requiring the Israelites to give to the land a beneficence similar to what they gave their slaves. The situation where the land is overworked is envisaged, and God, as the landlord, turns out his irresponsible tenants. In Genesis 2 human responsibility toward the land is expressed when Adam is given the task of "working and keeping" the garden of Eden. The same language is used of the responsibility of Israelite priests toward the temple, suggesting that Adam exercises a priestly role toward the garden. Humanity in general and Israel in particular are called to demonstrate a responsibility toward their environment. In the Old Testament, caring for the land is primarily expressed through food production since, in the ancient world, land means food. The modern call for organic approaches to food production is not only a dietary matter, but also a call to responsible land management.[22]

The production of food is not the result of autonomous human activity. The book of Deuteronomy expresses the point beautifully. "The land that you are entering to occupy is not like the land of Egypt, from where you have come, where you sow your seed and water by foot like a vegetable garden. Rather the land that you are crossing over to occupy is a land of hills and valleys, watered by rain from the heavens, a land that YHWH, your God, cares for" (Deut. 11:10-12). As a result the people of Israel must respond in faithful obedience to God's commands, for it is God who ensures the success of the harvest. When the harvest is received the Israelites are to respond in thankfulness. Many of the psalms express thankfulness to the God who provides food for all creation: "O give thanks to YHWH . . . who gives food to all flesh" (Ps. 136:1, 25). In Deuteronomy the feast of weeks and the feast of tabernacles are occasions of joyful feasting where some of the harvest produce is presented in thankfulness to God.

Appropriate attitudes to food are also to be expressed in its use. As is well known, the Old Testament makes frequent references to hospitality. Abraham, the primogenitor of the Israelites, is celebrated as an exemplary provider of hospitality in Genesis 18. In contrast, those who occupied the Transjordan and the area around the Dead Sea are frequently characterized as inhospitable (Gen. 19; Deut. 23; 2 Sam. 10). Although it is common to read of hospitality as a common practice of Middle Eastern peoples, the book of Deuteronomy presents generous hospitality with food as a defining national characteristic of the Israelites. It is to be expressed toward the marginalized in society — the orphan, the widow, the resident alien, and the Levite. Such generosity is ultimately derived from the character of God, who expressed generosity to the Israelites when they were in Egypt and in the wilderness (Deut. 10). In those texts, what matters is not so much what food one eats, but what is done with it.

Yet what one eats is not unimportant, at least for some parts of the Old Testament, though what this means is quite different from the concerns of the "biblical diets." Books such as Esther and Daniel, together with Judith in the Apocrypha, commend moderation as a Jewish characteristic in contrast to what they perceive as Persian overindulgence. This is especially apparent in Esther where the book opens with a baroque feast that lasts 180 days. In the book Xerxes and Haman are lovers of feasts, while the book's heroes, Esther and Mordechai, are characterized by their fasting. One finds a similar celebration of denial in the face of courtly indulgence in the book of Daniel. Daniel and his friends refuse the rich food of the Babylonian court and are sustained on the modest diet of vegetables and water (Dan. 1). This is not just an ethic of denial, but also an ethic of moderation. In the conclusion of the book of Esther the Jews celebrate a feast, for feasts do have a place. Purim, however, lasts a single day, providing a striking contrast with the 180-day feast that opened the book.

In the Old Testament — as also in the New — food and the body matter. What is eaten matters — albeit for different reasons than those to which biblical diets appeal — but also what is done with what is eaten matters. The Old Testament presses for food to be grown responsibly, received with thankfulness and rejoicing, given generously to others, and enjoyed in moderation.

Endnotes

Chapter 1: A Land Flowing with Milk and Honey

1. Josephus, *Jewish War* 3.49-50 (translation according to Josephus, *The Jewish War, Books I-III*, trans. H. St. J. Thackeray [London: William Heinemann, 1927]).

2. J. Wilkinson, *Jerusalem Pilgrims: Before the Crusades*, 2nd ed. (Warminster: Aris and Phillips, 2002), pp. 97-98.

3. Wilkinson, *Jerusalem Pilgrims*, pp. 94-98, 216-30.

4. Cited in C. Dauphin, "Plenty or Just Enough? The Diet of the Rural and Urban Masses of Byzantine Palestine," *Bulletin of the Anglo-Israel Archaeological Society* 17 (1999): 39-65, here 39. See Wilkinson, *Jerusalem Pilgrims*, p. 132.

5. Note the comment by R. E. Clements: "the land is not particularly fertile, but appeared so in contrast to the half-arid desert regions where the sheep-rearing Israelites had been accustomed to seek their pasture" (*Exodus*, Cambridge Bible Commentary [Cambridge: Cambridge University Press, 1972], p. 24).

6. M. Lichtheim, *Ancient Egyptian Literature: A Book of Readings*, vol. 1, *The Old and Middle Kingdoms* (Berkeley: University of California Press, 1973), pp. 226-27.

7. O. Borowski, *Agriculture in Ancient Israel* (Winona Lake, Ind.: Eisenbrauns, 1987), p. 3. It should be noted that the description of the land of Canaan as "a land flowing with milk and honey" is of questionable relevance to an account of *agriculture* in ancient Israel. The land's natural abundance in this idealistic vision is independent of human labor to extract food from the soil. In contrast, Lohfink writes, "one problem is that the well-being and wealth is painted in colors that really do not fit the land of Israel" (N. Lohfink, "'I Am Yahweh, Your Physician' [Exodus 15:26]: God, Society and Human Health in a Postexilic Revision of the Pentateuch [Exod. 15:2b, 26]," in *Theology of the Pentateuch: Themes of the Priestly Narrative and Deuteronomy* [Edinburgh: T. & T. Clark, 1994], pp. 35-95, here p. 84 n. 137).

8. O. Borowski, *Daily Life in Biblical Times* (Atlanta: SBL, 2003), p. 63.

9. P. J. King and L. Stager, *Life in Biblical Israel*, Library of Ancient Israel (Louisville: Westminster John Knox, 2001), pp. 85-107.

10. For discussion, see Richard A. Freund, "The Land Which Bled Forth Its Bounty: An Exile Image of the Land of Israel," *Scandinavian Journal of Theology* 13 (1999): 284-97; H. Ausloos, "'A Land Flowing with Milk and Honey': Indicative of a Deuteronomistic Redaction?" *Ephemerides theologicae lovanienses* 75 (1999): 297-314.

11. Ausloos, "A Land Flowing with Milk and Honey"; contra E. Levine, "The Land of Milk and Honey," *Journal for the Study of the Old Testament* 87 (2000): 43-57.

12. Ausloos, "Land Flowing," p. 301.

13. Contrast Ausloos, who writes, "One of the most characteristic expressions for denoting the Promised Land in the entire Old Testament, however, is the expression 'a land flowing with milk and honey'" ("Land Flowing," p. 297).

14. Exod. 3:8, 17; 13:5; 33:3; Lev. 20:24; Num. 16:13, 14; Deut. 6:3; 11:9; 26:9; 27:3; 31:20.

15. Jer. 11:5; 32:22; Ezek. 20:6, 15; Sir. 46:8; Bar. 1:20. J. D. M. Derrett also observes that the expression is rare in the postbiblical period ("Whatever Happened to the Land Flowing with Milk and Honey?" *Vigiliae Christianae* 38 [1984]: 178-84).

16. This appears to have been missed by the many scholars who consider whether the expression can be taken as evidence of a Deuteronomistic redaction in the books of Exodus to Numbers, e.g., Ausloos, "A Land Flowing with Milk and Honey"; B. R. Knipping, "Die Wortkombination 'Land, Fließend Milch und Honig': Eine kurze Problematisierung ihrer Ausdeutung, ihrer Überlieferungsgeschichte und der Tragweite eines Pentateuchmodells," *Biblische Notizen* 98 (1999): 55-71.

17. This might form an interesting parallel to Ezek. 20, where Ausloos argues that the bountiful land is deferred to a future date. "Its author reacts against the positive view on the taking possession of the Promised Land and gives a quite negative presentation of Israel's history. The 'land of milk and honey' will be something for the future" ("Land Flowing," p. 314).

18. M. Weinfeld, *Deuteronomy 1–11: A New Translation with Introduction and Commentary*, Anchor Bible 5 (New York: Doubleday, 1991), p. 392.

19. P. Garnsey, *Food and Society in Classical Antiquity*, Key Themes in Ancient History (Cambridge: Cambridge University Press, 1999), pp. 12-21.

Chapter 2: Reconstructing the Israelite Diet

1. J. Goody, *Cooking, Cuisine, and Class: A Study in Comparative Sociology*, Themes in the Social Sciences (Cambridge: Cambridge University Press, 1982). Schmitt adds "selection" to Goody's list. This allows her to discuss the dietary laws in Lev. 11 (E. Schmitt, *Das Essen in der Bibel: Literaturethnologische Aspekte des Alltäglichen*, Studien zur Kulturanthropologie 2 [Münster: LitVerlag, 1994]). Goody would probably have considered this under "social context," rather than as a stage in the food process. I doubt whether selection is a useful category for discussing food in the context of an-

cient Israel. It suggests a supermarket mentality that would have been alien to the Israelites.

2. Y. Aharoni, *Arad Inscriptions* (Jerusalem: Israel Exploration Society, 1981), pp. 11-118, 141-51; A. F. Rainey, "Three Additional Texts," in *Arad Inscriptions*; J. Naveh, "The Aramaic Ostraca from Tel Arad," in *Arad Inscriptions*; G. A. Reisner, C. S. Fisher, and D. G. Lyon, *Harvard Excavations at Samaria, 1908-1910*, vol. 1 (Cambridge: Harvard University Press, 1924), pp. 227-46; B. Rosen, "Wine and Oil Allocations in the Samaria Ostraca," *Tel Aviv* 13-14 (1986-87): 39-45.

3. Cf. K. W. Whitelam, *The Invention of Ancient Israel: The Silencing of Palestinian History* (London: Routledge, 1996).

Chapter 3: The Mediterranean Triad: Bread, Wine, and Oil

1. Y. Aharoni, *Arad Inscriptions* (Jerusalem: Israel Exploration Society, 1981); cf. B. Rosen, "Wine and Oil Allocations in the Samaria Ostraca," *Tel Aviv* 13-14 (1986-87): 39-45.

2. It is impossible to provide exact quantities for ancient societies, and this is especially the case for ancient Israel. But it is worth outlining some of the comparative evidence that may inform our understanding of the role of cereals in the Israelite diet. The ration lists from Egypt and Mesopotamia consistently indicate the prominence of cereals (see, e.g., R. Ellison, "Diet in Mesopotamia: The Evidence of the Barley Ration Texts [c. 3000-1400 B.C.]," *Iraq* 43 [1981]: 35-45). For the diet of Roman Palestine, Magen Broshi takes the food ration that the Talmud required be given to an estranged wife as representative. On this basis he calculates that "bread supplied half the daily calories (53-55 per cent)." This compares favorably with the proportions consumed by the modern Arab population in Israel and Palestine (M. Broshi, "The Diet of Palestine in the Roman Period: Introductory Notes," in *Bread, Wine, Walls, and Scrolls*, ed. M. Broshi, Journal for the Study of the Pseudepigrapha, Supplement Series 36 [London: Sheffield Academic, 2001], pp. 121-43, here p. 123). On the other hand, Foxhall and Forbes suggest a figure of from 70 to 75 percent for the Roman Empire (L. Foxhall and H. A. Forbes, "*Sitometreia*: The Role of Grain as a Staple Food in Classical Antiquity," *Chiron* 12 [1982]: 41-90). Either figure is far higher than bread consumption in modern Western economies.

3. Borowski also lists millet among the cereals cultivated in Iron Age Israel (Borowski, *Agriculture in Ancient Israel* [Winona Lake, Ind.: Eisenbrauns, 1987], pp. 92-93). A couple of Hebrew hapax legomena have been identified with millet: *dochan* is included in the mixture Ezekiel is commanded to make into a cake (Ezek. 4:9; Ludwig Koehler and Walter Baumgartner, eds., *The Hebrew and Aramaic Lexicon of the Old Testament*, 2 vols. [Leiden: Brill, 2000], pp. 218-19; hereafter KBL); *pannag* is on a list of agricultural products from Palestine (Ezek. 27:17 NRSV). Borowski notes that no archaeological evidence for millet has yet been discovered in Iron Age Palestine. Zohary and Hopf note that "signs of the cultivation of *P. miliaceum* in the Near East appear late.

The first known deposit of identifiable grains come from 700 BC Nimrud, Iraq" (D. Zohary and M. Hopf, *Domestication of Plants in the Old World: The Origin and Spread of Cultivated Plants in West Asia, Europe, and the Nile Valley*, 2nd ed. [Oxford: Clarendon, 1994], p. 80). Millet was, therefore, a late addition to the Israelite diet, and plays at most only a minor role in the Old Testament.

4. It has often been suggested that the festival of unleavened bread was associated with the beginning of the barley harvest, but a date in the month of Abib (March-April) would still see the barley being too immature to be harvested. For a review of the arguments, see A. D. H. Mayes, *Deuteronomy*, New Century Bible (London: Oliphants, 1979), pp. 254-57. Occasionally the assumption of this older view can be found, e.g., J. A. Soggin, *Israel in the Biblical Period: Institutions, Festivals, Ceremonies, Rituals*, trans. J. Bowden (Edinburgh: T. & T. Clark, 2001), pp. 93-94.

5. M. E. Kislev, "The Identification of *Hitta* and *Kussemet*," *Leshonenu* 37 (1973): 83-95, 243-52.

6. Zohary and Hopf, *Domestication of Plants*, p. 39; J. M. Renfrew, *Palaeoethnobotany: The Prehistoric Food Plants of the Near East and Europe* (London: Methuen, 1973), pp. 65-66.

7. The structure of the agricultural year in ancient Israel is set out in detail in the famous Gezer calendar. For a discussion of the Gezer calendar and agriculture, see Borowski, *Agriculture in Ancient Israel*, pp. 31-44.

8. Borowski misleadingly cites Renfrew, who writes, "moderately heavy rain in early summer when the shoots are in full growth and ears developing is most beneficial, but heavy autumn and winter rains greatly retard the development of the plant and result in a small grain yield" (Borowski, *Agriculture in Ancient Israel*, p. 89, citing Renfrew, *Palaeoethnobotany*, p. 65). However, Renfrew's observations draw on research undertaken at Rothamsted, Hertfordshire, and thus concern bread wheat (*Triticum aestivum*) grown according to a northern continental season.

9. Borowski, *Agriculture in Ancient Israel*, p. 89.

10. Zohary and Hopf, *Domestication of Plants*, p. 46. The identification of *kussemet* with emmer wheat rather than spelt (see, e.g., KBL, p. 490) was argued by Kislev, "The Identification of *Hitta* and *Kussemet*." As Zohary and Hopf note (pp. 41-42), emmer is native to Palestine, while spelt is a form of bread wheat (*Triticum aestivum*) and is more suited to a continental climate. *Kussemet* is mentioned only three times in the Old Testament: Exod. 9:32; Isa. 28:25; Ezek. 4:9. Exod. 9:32, of course, refers to crop cultivation in Egypt.

11. Broshi, "Diet of Palestine," p. 124; D. Baly, *The Geography of Palestine: A Study in Historical Geography* (London: Lutterworth, 1957), pp. 140, 218, 237.

12. Barley was the main cereal crop in Mesopotamia where saline soils had resulted from long reliance on irrigation (Broshi, "Diet of Palestine," p. 125).

13. The low status of barley in the Roman Empire is well known. It is often thought that the same judgment held for classical Greece, though this may not be the case (P. Garnsey, *Food and Society in Classical Antiquity*, Key Themes in Ancient History [Cambridge: Cambridge University Press, 1999], pp. 119-20).

14. Broshi, "Diet of Palestine," p. 125.

15. The Hebrew term *solet* should be translated as "fine flour" (KBL, pp. 758-59; G. Dalman, *Arbeit und Sitte in Palästina, III: Von der Ernte zum Mahl*, 7 vols. [Hildesheim: Georg Olms, 1964 (1933)], pp. 292-93; cf. LXX *semidalis*). An identification with wheat occurs in Exod. 29:2. Milgrom translates as "semolina," which is defined as "the grain-like portions of wheat retained in the bolting machine after the fine flour has been passed through" (J. Milgrom, *Leviticus 1–16*, Anchor Bible 3 [New York: Doubleday, 1991], p. 179). This is on the basis of a somewhat opaque aphorism in the Mishnah (*m. Avot* 5:15) where one type of Torah reader is compared to "a strainer — for he lets out the wine and keeps in the lees" and another type to "a sifter — for he lets out the flour and keeps in the *solet*." However, other rabbinic evidence does not support Milgrom, for the finest flour that results from a series of siftings is described as the *solet*. In *t. Menahot* 8:14 and *m. Menahot* 6:7 the final sifting results in the *solet* remaining in the strainer, and one must presume that what passes through the sift is worthless powder. This explains the Mishnah's aphorism because the pattern established in earlier aphorisms is that the "strainer" is a positive category, and the "sifter" is entirely negative (J. Neusner, *Torah from Our Sages: Pirke Avot* [Chappaqua, N.Y.: Rossel Books, 1983], pp. 162-63). Thus, the strainer is praiseworthy because what comes through the strainer is wine. On the other hand, what the sifter produces is utterly worthless, which would not be the case if semolina was being sifted from fine flour (I. Epstein, *The Babylonian Talmud: Seder Nezikin — Aboth* [London: Soncino Press, 1935], pp. 69-70 n. 10). For the same comparison of straining wine and sifting flour see *y. Shabbat* 7.

16. In particular we should notice that the use of barley, rather than wheat, marks one of many contrasts with the Nazirite (Num. 6:15). Also unusual is the lack of oil, which is paralleled only in the purification offering (Lev. 5:11). On the other hand, Davies offers a historical explanation when he speculates that the use of barley in offerings reflects earlier cultic practice (E. W. Davies, *Numbers*, New Century Bible [London: Marshall Pickering, 1995], p. 52; cf. G. B. Gray, *Numbers*, International Critical Commentary [Edinburgh: T. & T. Clark, 1912], p. 50). Note also that barley is connected to nefarious cultic acts in Ezek. 13:19.

17. For *se'orim* as barley flour, see KBL, p. 1346.

18. *m. Ketubbot* 5:8 (Broshi, "Diet of Palestine," p. 124).

19. Barley is nowhere else described as animal fodder in the Old Testament. Usually straw *(teben)* was used (Gen. 24:25, 32; Judg. 19:19; Isa. 11:7; 65:25). This is probably part of the utopian portrayal of Solomon's reign in 1 Kings. In this respect it is worth observing that only flour *(qemach)* and choice flour *(solet)* are listed among the provisions of Solomon's table. As for barley and wheat, we would add that wheat is always listed before barley (e.g., Isa. 28:25, Ezek. 4:9), though this may simply be a matter of euphony.

20. Josephus, *Jewish War* 5.427.

21. See G. Dalman, *Arbeit und Sitte in Palästina, IV: Brot, Öl und Wein*, 7 vols. (Hildesheim: Georg Olms, 1964 [1935]), pp. 1-152.

22. Broshi, "Diet of Palestine," p. 125.

23. R. I. Curtis, *Ancient Food Technology,* Technology and Change in History 5 (Leiden: Brill, 2001), p. 207.

24. M. Broshi, "Wine in Ancient Palestine: Introductory Notes," in *Bread, Wine, Walls, and Scrolls.*

25. T. Unwin, *Wine and the Vine: An Historical Geography of Viticulture and the Wine Trade* (London: Routledge, 1991).

26. "The earliest definite signs of *Vitis* cultivation come from Chaleolithic and from Early Bronze Age sites in the Levant" (Zohary and Hopf, *Domestication of Plants,* p. 148). The wild *Vitis silvestris* may have been domesticated in Anatolia or in a number of independent locations. The relative proximity of one of the likely places of domestication and Noah's Mount Ararat occasionally leads scholars into unguarded comparisons: "The biblical tradition that Noah planted a vineyard after the flood (Gen 9.20) suggests that the biblical writers were aware of the antiquity of viticulture and the location of domestication of the vine" (Borowski, *Agriculture in Ancient Israel,* p. 102) or "it is possible that Gen 8:4 reflects an ancient tradition that recalls the origin of the vine" (C. E. Walsh, *The Fruit of the Vine: Viticulture in Ancient Israel,* Harvard Semitic Monographs 60 [Winona Lake, Ind.: Eisenbrauns, 2000], p. 13). How these ideas square with what is known about transmission of oral knowledge is not explained.

27. For analysis see Walsh, *Fruit of the Vine,* pp. 87-126; V. H. Matthews, "Treading the Winepress: Actual and Metaphorical Viticulture in the Ancient Near East," in *Food and Drink in the Biblical Worlds,* ed. A. Brenner and J. W. van Henten, Semeia 86 (Atlanta: Society of Biblical Literature, 1999), pp. 19-32.

28. Walsh, *Fruit of the Vine,* pp. 115-16.

29. See S. Dar, *Landscape and Pattern: An Archaeological Survey of Samaria, 800 BCE–636 CE,* 2 vols. (Oxford: BAR, 1986), 1:153-58; Walsh, *Fruit of the Vine,* pp. 187-92.

30. Broshi assumes that wine was diluted in the Roman period ("Wine in Ancient Palestine," pp. 161-62).

31. Dar, *Landscape and Pattern,* pp. 160-61; cf. Broshi, "Wine in Ancient Palestine," esp. p. 162.

32. For discussion see J. M. Sasson, "The Blood of Grapes: Viticuture and Intoxication in the Hebrew Bible," in *Drinking in Ancient Societies: History and Culture of Drinks in the Ancient Near East,* ed. L. Milano, History of the Ancient Near East Studies 6 (Padua: Sargon, 1994), pp. 399-419. Walsh suggests "date wine" (*Fruit of the Vine,* pp. 201-2). However, while dates and date wine were common in Egypt and Mesopotamia, they were cultivated only in a small area of Palestine. *Shekar,* on the other hand, occurs on a number of occasions in the Old Testament.

33. L. E. Stager, "First Fruits of Civilization," in *Palestine in the Bronze and Iron Age: Papers in Honour of Olga Tufnell,* ed. J. N. Tubb (London: Institute of Archaeology, 1985), pp. 172-87.

34. L. E. Stager, "Ashkelon and the Archaeology of Destruction: Kislev 604 BCE," *Eretz Israel* 25 (1996): 61-74; J. B. Pritchard, *Winery, Defenses, and Soundings at Gibeon* (Philadelphia: Pennsylvania University Museum, 1964).

35. R. Frankel, *Wine and Oil Production in Antiquity in Israel and Other Mediterra-*

nean Countries, JSOT/ASOR Monograph Series 10 (Sheffield: Sheffield Academic, 1999), pp. 43-46; F. S. Frick, "'Oil from Flinty Rock' (Deuteronomy 32:13): Olive Cultivation and Olive Oil Processing in the Hebrew Bible — a Socio-Materialist Perspective," in *Food and Drink in the Biblical Worlds*, pp. 1-17, here pp. 11-13.

36. Borowski, *Agriculture in Ancient Israel*, p. 123.

37. Renfrew, *Palaeoethnobotany*, pp. 133-34.

38. R. Frankel, "Ancient Oil Mills and Presses in the Land of Israel," in *History and Technology of Olive Oil in the Holy Land*, ed. E. Ayalon (Tel Aviv: Eretz Israel Museum, 1994), pp. 19-89, here p. 22.

39. Those olives that remained were, according to the Deuteronomic legislator, to be left for the poor (Deut. 24:20). Frankel notes that the procedure is the opposite of that suggested by Varro and the Mishnah (*m. Hallah* 3:9; Frankel, *Wine and Oil Production*, p. 37).

40. "Treading olives" is mentioned in Mic. 6:15. Although Dalman thought this was not to be understood literally, recent writers note comparative evidence for treading olives (Frankel, *Wine and Oil Production*, p. 46).

41. Curtis, *Ancient Food Technology*, p. 227.

42. "There is clear evidence for the use of beam and weights presses in Syria and Cyprus during the Late Bronze Age and it is possible that such presses were in use in Crete even earlier. In Israel, however, this technique was apparently not introduced before Iron Age I. Only one complete lever and weights press has been published from this period, from Dan at the very north of the country, but large numbers are known throughout the country from Iron Age II" (Frankel, *Wine and Oil Production*, p. 62).

43. For a description of the archaeological evidence and illustrations, see Frankel, *Wine and Oil Production in Antiquity in Israel and Other Mediterranean Countries*; Curtis, *Ancient Food Technology*, pp. 226-33.

44. Broshi, "Diet of Palestine," p. 122. The amount of oil to be provided depends on the conversion rate used.

45. Dar, *Landscape and Pattern*, p. 161. Zertal suggests a high figure (A. Zertal, "The Cultivation and the Economy of Olives during the Iron Age I in the Hill Country of Manasseh," in *Olive Oil in Antiquity: Israel and Neighbouring Countries from the Neolithic to the Early Arab Period*, ed. D. Eitam and M. Heltzer, History of the Ancient Near East Studies 7 [Padua: Sargon, 1996], pp. 307-14).

46. Frankel, *Wine and Oil Production*, p. 45.

Chapter 4: Vegetables, Pulses, and Fruit

1. The low opinion of vegetables continues to be found in some rabbinic texts. In *b. Pesahim* 42a coarse bread, new beer, and raw vegetables are considered unhealthy, while sifted bread, fat meat, and old wine are considered beneficial (M. J. Geller, "Diet and Regimen in the Babylonian Diet," in *Food and Identity in the Ancient World*, ed.

C. Grottanelli and L. Milano, History of the Ancient Near East Studies 9 [Padua: Sargon, 2004], pp. 217-42).

2. Unfortunately archaeology can make little contribution to this problem, as vegetables rarely leave any remains (D. Zohary and M. Hopf, *Domestication of Plants in the Old World: The Origin and Spread of Cultivated Plants in West Asia, Europe, and the Nile Valley,* 2nd ed. [Oxford: Clarendon, 1994], p. 181).

3. Rosen notes that "there is occasional evidence of the use of wild plants in the Iron Age. Traces of *Malva* sp. in Beer-Sheba attest to their role as contributors of calories and vitamins to the nutritional intake of the contemporary peasant" (B. Rosen, "Subsistence Economy in Iron Age I," in *From Nomadism to Monarchy: Archaeological and Historical Aspects of Ancient Israel,* ed. I. Finkelstein and N. Na'aman [Jerusalem: Israel Exploration Society, 1994], pp. 339-51, here p. 342).

On the Roman period, Broshi observes that "a considerable number of the vegetables consumed in our period . . . were wild (as they are for the modern Palestinian Arab peasant) . . . a close reading of the Talmudic literature and of modern ethnobotanical literature reveals the important contribution of wild vegetables to the diet" (Broshi, "The Diet of Palestine in the Roman Period: Introductory Notes," in *Bread, Wine, Walls, and Scrolls,* ed. M. Broshi, Journal for the Study of the Pseudepigrapha, Supplement Series 36 [London: Sheffield Academic, 2001], p. 131; cf. J. M. Frayn, *Subsistence Farming in Roman Italy* [London: Centaur Press, 1979]). To a large degree the use of wild plants by the Israelites to supplement their diet is a matter of critical conjecture because of limited sources. For another ancient society for which there is greater literary evidence, see J. M. Frayn, "Wild and Cultivated Plants: A Note on the Peasant Economy of Roman Italy," *Journal of Roman Studies* 65 (1975): 32-39.

4. Zohary and Hopf, *Domestication of Plants,* pp. 88-94.

5. J. M. Renfrew, *Palaeoethnobotany: The Prehistoric Food Plants of the Near East and Europe* (London: Methuen, 1973), pp. 108-9.

6. Renfrew, *Palaeoethnobotany,* p. 111.

7. Zohary and Hopf, *Domestication of Plants,* p. 95.

8. Renfrew, *Palaeoethnobotany,* p. 119. O. Borowski, *Agriculture in Ancient Israel* (Winona Lake, Ind.: Eisenbrauns, 1987), p. 95, identifies *chamits* in Isa. 30:24 with chickpeas. On the other hand, Ludwig Koehler and Walter Baumgartner, eds., *The Hebrew and Aramaic Lexicon of the Old Testament,* 2 vols. (Leiden: Brill, 2000), p. 328, identify it with "sorrel" (i.e., *rumex*). The former is related to Arabic *ḥummuṣ* and the latter to Arabic *ḥummaḍ*. The earlier translation "seasoned" or "rich" still enjoys some support (e.g., J. Blenkinsopp, *Isaiah 1–39,* Anchor Bible 19 [New York: Doubleday, 2000], p. 419; J. D. W. Watts, *Isaiah 1–33,* Word Biblical Commentary 24 [Waco: Word, 1985], p. 401, though Watts's argument that "בליל implies a treatment of some kind" appears confused). See also H. Wildberger, *Jesaja,* Biblischer Kommentar Altes Testament 10/3 (Neukirchen-Vluyn: Neukirchener Verlag, 1982), p. 1202, and L. Köhler, "Jes 30,24 בליל חמיץ," *Zeitschrift für die alttestamentliche Wissenschaft* 40 (1922): 15-17.

9. Zohary and Hopf, *Domestication of Plants,* p. 111.

10. Zohary and Hopf, *Domestication of Plants,* p. 116.

11. Köhler, "Jes 30,24 בליל חמיץ."

12. "While it can be safely assumed that legumes were cultivated to some extent by the Iron Age I peasant, little if any data are available on this point" (Rosen, "Subsistence Economy in Iron Age I," p. 342).

13. For the rest of the Roman Empire, compare also the comments by P. Garnsey, *Food and Society in Classical Antiquity,* Key Themes in Ancient History (Cambridge: Cambridge University Press, 1999), p. 15.

14. Broshi cites Y. Feliks, "Jewish Agriculture in the Period of the Mishnah," in *Eretz Israel from the Destruction of the Second Temple to the Muslim Conquests,* ed. Z. Baras (Jerusalem: Yad Ben Zvi, 1982), pp. 419-41, esp. pp. 426, 429-30.

15. Broshi, "Diet of Palestine," p. 122.

16. Zohary and Hopf, *Domestication of Plants,* p. 86; Renfrew, *Palaeoethnobotany,* pp. 113-15.

17. K. D. White, *Roman Farming: Aspects of Greek and Roman Life* (Ithaca, N.Y.: Cornell University Press, 1970), pp. 113, 121-23.

18. Borowski's appeal to the prohibition against sowing a field with two kinds of seeds (Lev. 19:19; Deut. 22:9) as possible evidence of crop rotation is unlikely (*Agriculture in Ancient Israel,* pp. 149-51).

19. Borowski, however, assumes its practicability (*Agriculture in Ancient Israel,* pp. 144-45). Cf. J. Milgrom, *Leviticus 23–27: A New Translation with Introduction and Commentary,* Anchor Bible 3B (New York: Doubleday, 2001), pp. 2248-52; D. C. Hopkins, *The Highlands of Canaan: Agricultural Life in the Early Iron Age,* Social World of Biblical Antiquity 3 (Sheffield: JSOT Press, 1985), pp. 200-202.

20. Hopkins, *The Highlands of Canaan,* p. 197. Hopkins has an excellent discussion of crop rotation (pp. 192-202).

21. Garnsey notes for Attica the possibility of failure in the legume crop to be three years in every four (P. Garnsey, *Famine and Food Supply in the Graeco-Roman World: Response to Risk and Crisis* [Cambridge: Cambridge University Press, 1990]).

22. Pliny describes how bean meal was added to flour to increase the weight of loaves (*Natural History* 18.30; cited in Renfrew, *Palaeoethnobotany,* p. 109).

23. C. Dauphin rightly lists fruit under "rare delicacies" in a discussion of Byzantine diet (Dauphin, "Plenty or Just Enough? The Diet of the Rural and Urban Masses of Byzantine Palestine," *Bulletin of the Anglo-Israel Archaeological Society* 17 [1999]: 39-65).

24. For the translation of *debash* as "fruit syrup," rather than honey, see chapter 6.

25. Renfrew, *Palaeoethnobotany,* p. 135.

26. Borowski, *Agriculture in Ancient Israel,* p. 114.

27. Broshi, "Diet of Palestine," p. 122. For the role of figs in the economy of Roman Syria, see F. M. Heichelheim, "Roman Syria," in *An Economic Survey of Ancient Rome,* ed. T. Frank (Baltimore: Johns Hopkins Press, 1938), pp. 121-257, here p. 136.

28. R. C. Steiner, *Stockmen from Tekoa, Sycomores from Sheba,* Catholic Biblical Quarterly, Monograph Series 36 (Washington, D.C.: Catholic Biblical Association of America, 2003), p. 46.

29. Ripening of the fruit is achieved through gashing the skin, which produces ethylene gas (J. Galil, "An Ancient Technique for Ripening Sycomore Fruit in East Mediterranean Countries," *Economic Botany* 22 [1966]: 178-90). This process is often associated with the description of Amos's profession as *boles shiqmim* (Amos 7:14). For the most recent discussion and detailed bibliography, see Steiner, *Stockmen from Tekoa, Sycomores from Sheba*. Galil suggests that "in ancient Israel, sycomore was eaten mostly by the poor who could not afford the more expensive fruit" (Galil, p. 178). This is a reasonable assumption, but Galil offers no argument.

30. On Jericho and its palms, see J. R. Bartlett, *Jericho* (London: Lutterworth, 1982), pp. 18-20. For a discussion of the date, see A. Goor, "The History of the Date through the Ages in the Holy Land," *Economic Botany* 21 (1967): 320-40.

31. Goor gives the pomegranate a larger role in the Israelite diet. For a wider discussion of pomegranates, see A. Goor, "The History of the Pomegranate in the Holy Land," *Economic Botany* 21 (1967): 215-29.

32. Borowski, *Agriculture in Ancient Israel*, pp. 129-30. See also I. Löw, *Die Flora der Juden*, 4 vols. (Hildesheim: Georg Olms, 1967 [1924]), 3:212-35, cf. pp. 155-59, 240-44.

33. Zohary and Hopf, *Domestication of Plants*, pp. 172-73.

34. Zohary and Hopf, *Domestication of Plants*, p. 166.

Chapter 5: Meat, Milk, Birds, and Fish

1. J. Bottéro, *Textes Culinaires Mésopotamiens: Mesopotamian Culinary Texts*, Mesopotamian Civilizations 6 (Winona Lake, Ind.: Eisenbrauns, 1995); Bottéro, "The Most Ancient Recipe of All," in *Food in Antiquity*, ed. J. Wilkens, D. Harvey, and M. Dobson (Exeter: University of Exeter Press, 1995), pp. 248-55; Bottéro, "The Cuisine of Ancient Mesopotamia," *Biblical Archaeologist* 48 (1985): 36-47.

2. For summaries of archaeozoology and its results in the Levant, see E. B. Firmage, "Zoology (Fauna)," in *Anchor Bible Dictionary* (New York: Doubleday, 1992), 6:1109-67; B. Hesse and P. Wapnish, "An Archaeozoological Perspective on the Cultural Use of Mammals in the Levant," in *A History of the Animal World in the Ancient Near East*, ed. B. J. Collins, Handbook of Oriental Studies, Section 1, The Near and Middle East (Leiden: Brill, 2001), pp. 457-91.

3. P. Croft, "Archaeozoological Studies. Section A: The Osteological Remains (Mammalian and Avian)," in *The Renewed Archaeological Excavations at Lachish (1973-1994)*, vol. 5, ed. D. Ussishkin (Tel Aviv: Tel Aviv University, 2004), pp. 2254-2348; A. von den Driesch and J. Boessneck, "Final Report on the Zooarchaeological Investigation of Animal Bone Finds from Tell Hesban, Jordan," in *Faunal Remains*, ed. O. S. LaBianca and A. von den Driesch, Hesban 13 (Berrien Springs, Mich.: Andrews University Press, 1995), pp. 65-108, here p. 73.

4. Clutton-Brock traces the declining role of the gazelle in the food economy at Jericho from Pre-Pottery Neolithic B to the Byzantine period. Although the gazelle continued to be hunted into the Byzantine period, it had stopped playing an important

role in the economy after the Middle Bronze Age (J. Clutton-Brock, "The Primary Food Animals of the Jericho Tell from the Proto-Neolithic to the Byzantine Period," *Levant* 3 [1971]: 41-55).

5. L. K. Horwitz et al., "Faunal and Malacological Remains from the Middle Bronze, Late Bronze and Iron Age Levels at Tel Yoqneʿam," in *Yoqneʿam III: The Middle and Late Bronze Ages; Final Report of the Archaeological Excavations (1977-1988)*, ed. A. Ben-Tor, D. Ben-Ami, and A. Livneh, Qedem 7 (Jerusalem: Institute of Archaeology, Hebrew University of Jerusalem, 2005), pp. 395-435, here p. 404; L. K. Horwitz and I. Milevski, "The Faunal Evidence for Socioeconomic Change between the Middle and Late Bronze Age in the Southern Levant," in *Studies in the Archaeology of Israel and Neighbouring Lands: In Memory of Douglas L. Esse*, ed. S. R. Wolff, ASOR Books 5 (Chicago: Oriental Institute of the University of Chicago; Atlanta: American Schools of Oriental Research, 2001), pp. 283-305.

6. The utilization of wild animals is much lower in the south of the country than in the north. Larger finds of wild animals have been made at Dan (7 percent), Kinnoret (12 percent), Ebal (10.5 percent), and Bab el-Hawa (8 percent) (P. Wapnish and B. Hesse, "Faunal Remains from Tel Dan: Perspectives on Animal Production at a Village, Urban and Ritual Center," *Archaeozoologia* 4 [1991]: 9-87; R. Ziegler and J. Boessneck, "Tierrest der Eisenzeit II," in *Kinneret: Ergebnisse der Ausgrabungen auf dem Tell El-ʿOrmeam, See Gennesaret 1982-1985*, ed. V. Fritz [Wiesbaden: Harrassowitz, 1990], pp. 133-58; L. K. Horwitz, "Faunal Remains from the Early Iron Age Site on Mount Ebal," *Tel Aviv* 13-14 [1986]: 173-89; O. Raphael and O. Lernau, "Faunal Remains from Bab-El-Hawa: An Iron Age–Byzantine Site in the Golan Heights," *Archaeozoologia* 8 [1996]: 105-18).

7. For these animals see Wapnish and Hesse, "Faunal Remains from Tel Dan"; S. Davis, "The Large Mammal Bones," in *Excavations at Tell Qasile: Part Two; The Philistine Sanctuary; Various Finds, the Pottery, Conclusions, Appendixes*, ed. A. Mazar, Qedem 20 (Jerusalem: Hebrew University of Jerusalem, 1985), pp. 148-50; Davis, "The Faunal Remains," in *Tell Qiri: A Village in the Jezreel Valley*, ed. A. Ben-Tor and Y. Portugali, Qedem 24 (Jerusalem: Hebrew University, 1987), pp. 249-51.

8. Strangely, in his analysis of diet in the Byzantine period, Dauphin fails to provide any detailed discussion of milk and dairy products (Dauphin, "Plenty or Just Enough? The Diet of the Rural and Urban Masses of Byzantine Palestine," *Bulletin of the Anglo-Israel Archaeological Society* 17 [1999]: 39-65)!

9. *b. Shabbat* 19b. See, further, Z. Safrai, *The Economy of Roman Palestine* (London: Routledge, 1994), p. 170.

10. The translation of *tson* as "sheep" in Isa. 7:21 (NRSV) could be misleading, unless the intention of the verse is that even the animals not usually preferred for milking will produce an uncharacteristically abundant supply.

11. G. Dalman, *Arbeit und Sitte in Palästina, VI: Zeltleben, Vieh- und Milchwirtschaft, Jagd, Fischfang*, 7 vols. (Hildesheim: Georg Olms, 1964 [1939]), pp. 180-203; Firmage, "Zoology (Fauna)," pp. 1126-29; C. Palmer, "'Following the Plough': The Agricultural Environment of Northern Jordan," *Levant* 30 (1998): 129-65, here p. 159.

12. O. Borowski, *Every Living Thing: Daily Use of Animals in Ancient Israel* (Walnut Creek, Calif.: AltaMira, 1998), p. 54.

13. For the technology of processing, see R. I. Curtis, *Ancient Food Technology,* Technology and Change in History 5 (Leiden: Brill, 2001), pp. 234-38.

14. M. Stol, "Milk, Butter and Cheese," *Bulletin of Sumerian Agriculture* 7 (1993): 99-113; cf. M. L. Ryder, "Sheep and Goat Husbandry with Particular Reference to Textile Fibre and Milk Production," *Bulletin of Sumerian Agriculture* 7 (1993): 9-32; and C. Palmer, "Milk and Cereals: Identifying Food and Food Identity among Fallāḥīn and Bedouin in Jordan," *Levant* 34 (2002): 173-95. Some groups in the Near East continue to produce a variety of dairy products with traditional methods. For a description of some of these, see Borowski, *Every Living Thing,* pp. 55-56, and Palmer, "Milk and Cereals."

15. Prov. 30:33 probably suggests that *chem'ah* is to be associated with butter (so A. Caquot, "חָלָב chālābh," in *Theological Dictionary of the Old Testament,* ed. G. J. Botterweck and H. Ringgren [Grand Rapids: Eerdmans, 1980], 4:386-91, here p. 390).

16. Note 1 Sam. 17:17-18, where David brings a gift of cheese for the captain of the unit, while the brothers are given bread.

17. This is a difficult text to translate. *'Atinaw* is a hapax legomenon that LXX and Vulgate render with "intestines" and Targ. with "pails." Pope emends to *'atimaw* and translates "flanks, haunches" (M. Pope, *Job,* Anchor Bible 15 [Garden City, N.Y.: Doubleday, 1965], p. 146). It is also common to read "fat" *(cheleb)* instead of "milk" *(chalab),* which involves just a change in pointing.

18. For significant remains see L. K. Horwitz and E. Tchernov, "Subsistence Patterns in Ancient Jerusalem: A Study of Animal Remains from the Ophel," in *Excavations in the South of the Temple Mount: The Ophel of Biblical Jerusalem,* ed. E. Mazar and B. Mazar, Qedem 29 (Jerusalem: Hebrew University of Jerusalem, 1989), pp. 144-54; Horwitz and Tchernov, "Bird Remains from Areas A, D, H and K," in *Excavations at the City of David, 1978-1985,* vol. 4, *Various Reports,* ed. D. T. Ariel and A. de Groot, Qedem 35 (Jerusalem: Hebrew University, 1996), pp. 298-301; Croft, "Archaeozoological Studies."

19. S. Hellwing, M. Sadeh, and V. Kishon, "Faunal Remains," in *Shiloh: The Archaeology of a Biblical Site,* ed. I. Finkelstein (Tel Aviv: Tel Aviv University, 1993), pp. 309-50.

20. Hesse and Wapnish, "An Archaeozoological Perspective on the Cultural Use of Mammals in the Levant."

21. This was first proposed by Taran in 1975. "I presume that the cocks of ancient Judea, during the time of the First Temple and a few centuries afterwards, were all, or at least mostly, of the fighting type. The fact that the egg as a food is nowhere mentioned in all the Old Testament lends weight to this supposition. In fact, Judea was in an area where fighting birds were much preferred as late as the first century AD. Aldrovandi quoted Varro, Pliny and Collumlea who praised several breeds of chickens for their pugnacious temper, among them the Median (Perse), the Rhodian (Rhodes) and Alexandrian (Egypt). The Talmud (Yevamor 84b) quoted Rabi Yehuda Hanasi (second century AD), mentions a breed of variety of fowls, named Beit Boyko, known for their dangerous fighting cocks" (M. Taran, "Early Records of the Domestic Fowl in Ancient

Judea," *Ibis* 117 [1975]: 109-10, here p. 110). This proposal does not seem to be well known and is worth consideration.

22. W. J. Stadelman, "Chicken Eggs," in *The Cambridge World History of Food*, ed. K. F. Kiple and K. C. Ornelas (Cambridge: Cambridge University Press, 2000), 1:499-508, here p. 500.

23. "And to come to the Mosaic legislation, many of the laws, so far as their literal observance is concerned, are clearly irrational, while others are impossible. An example of irrationality is the prohibition to eat vultures, seeing that nobody even in the worst famine was ever driven by want to the extremity of eating these creatures. . . . And if you would like to see some impossibilities that are enacted in the law, let us observe that the goatstag, which Moses commands us to offer in sacrifice as a clean animal, is a creature that cannot possibly exist; while as to the griffin, which the lawgiver forbids to be eaten, there is no record that it has even fallen into the hands of man" (Origen, *De principiis* 4.3.2 in the Greek; translation according to Origen, *On First Principles*, trans. G. W. Butterworth [New York: Harper and Row, 1966], pp. 290-91).

24. For a full discussion see O. Lernau and D. Golani, "Section B: The Osteological Remains (Aquatic)," in *The Renewed Archaeological Excavations at Lachish (1973-1994)*, esp. pp. 2486-87.

25. See W. Van Neer et al., "Fish Remains from Archaeological Sites as Indicators of Former Trade Connections in the Eastern Mediterranean," *Paléorient* 30 (2004): 101-48. Most fish remains from Israel have been examined by O. Lernau. See O. Lernau, "Fish Bones," in *Meggido III: The 1992-1996 Seasons*, vol. 2, ed. I. Finkelstein, D. Ussishkin, and B. Halpern (Tel Aviv: Tel Aviv University, 2000), pp. 463-77; H. Lernau and O. Lernau, "Fish Bone Remains," in *Excavations in the South of the Temple Mount: The Ophel of Biblical Jerusalem*, ed. E. Mazar and B. Mazar, Qedem 29 (Jerusalem: Hebrew University, 1989), pp. 155-61; H. Lernau and O. Lernau, "Fish Remains," in *Excavations at the City of David, 1978-1985: Stratigraphical, Environmental, and Other Reports*, ed. A. de Groot and D. T. Ariel, Qedem 33 (Jerusalem: Hebrew University, 1992), pp. 131-48; O. Lernau, "Fish Remains from Tel Harrasim," in *The Sixth Season of Excavation at Tel Harrasim (Nahal Barkai), 1995*, ed. S. Givon (Tel Aviv: Bar Ilan University, 1996), pp. 14*-23*; O. Lernau, "Fish Remains at Tel Harrasim," in *The Eleventh Season of Excavation at Tel Harrasim (Nahal Barkai), 2000*, ed. S. Givon (Tel Aviv: Bar Ilan University, 2002), pp. 4*-12*; O. Lernau, "Fish Bones from Horbat Rosh Zayit," in *Horbat Rosh Zayit: An Iron Age Storage Fort and Village*, ed. Z. Gal and Y. Alexandre, Israel Antiquities Authority Reports (Jerusalem: Israel Antiquities Authority, 2000), pp. 233-37; O. Lernau, "Fish Bones," in *Tel Kabri: The 1986-1993 Excavation Seasons*, ed. A. Kempinski (Tel Aviv: Tel Aviv University, 2002), pp. 409-27.

26. "The oldest evidence in the Levant for trade in Red Sea fish comes from the Iron Age II period, which represents a time of resettlement and fortification of the caravan routes in the Negev in order to attain access to the Red Sea incense and spice trade. During this time, Red Sea parrotfish appear at Tel Ashqelon, Tel Gerisa, and Tell Hesban" (Van Neer et al., "Fish Remains," p. 137).

27. Van Neer et al., "Fish Remains," p. 134.

28. "The relatively large selection of different fish, originating both from the Mediterranean Sea and from the River Jordan, and probably other rivers too, may suggest a high standard of living for at least some of the inhabitants of the city" (Lernau and Lernau, "Fish Remains," p. 136).

Chapter 6: Condiments and Other Foods

1. O. Borowski, *Agriculture in Ancient Israel* (Winona Lake, Ind.: Eisenbrauns, 1987), p. 99.

2. J. Milgrom, *Leviticus 1–16*, Anchor Bible 3 (New York: Doubleday, 1991), pp. 189-90.

3. A. Mazar, *The Tel Rehov Excavations — 2007*; available from http://www.rehov.org/bee.htm (accessed 10 October 2007). I am grateful to Amihai Mazar for drawing my attention to his discoveries in 2005.

4. G. Dalman, *Arbeit und Sitte in Palästina, IV: Brot, Öl und Wein*, 7 vols. (Hildesheim: Georg Olms, 1964 [1935]), p. 107; D. Brothwell and P. Brothwell, *Food in Antiquity: A Survey of the Diet of Early Peoples* (London: Thomas and Hudson, 1969), p. 77.

5. E. Neufeld, "Apiculture in Ancient Palestine (Early and Middle Iron Age) within the Framework of the Ancient Near East," *Ugarit-Forschungen* 10 (1978): 238-47, here p. 247.

6. M. Broshi, "The Diet of Palestine in the Roman Period: Introductory Notes," in *Bread, Wine, Walls, and Scrolls*, ed. M. Broshi, Journal for the Study of the Pseudepigrapha, Supplement Series 36 (London: Sheffield Academic, 2001), p. 138.

7. There is now archaeological evidence for the existence of cumin in Palestine (R. Neef, "Plants," in *Picking Up the Threads: A Continuing Review of Excavations at Deir Alla, Jordan*, ed. G. van der Kooij and M. M. Ibrahim [Leiden: University of Leiden Archaeological Centre, 1989], pp. 290-96; cf. Borowski, *Agriculture in Ancient Israel*, p. 97).

8. For condiments, see G. Dalman, *Arbeit und Sitte in Palästina, II: Der Ackerbau*, 7 vols. (Hildesheim: Georg Olms, 1964 [1932]), pp. 290-96. For salt, see Dalman, *Arbeit und Sitte in Palästina, IV*, pp. 49-58.

Chapter 7: Modeling the Israelite Diet

1. *m. Ketubbot* 5:8. Translation from J. Neusner, *Mishnah: A New Translation* (New Haven: Yale University Press, 1988).

2. M. Broshi, "The Diet of Palestine in the Roman Period: Introductory Notes," in *Bread, Wine, Walls, and Scrolls*, ed. M. Broshi, Journal for the Study of the Pseudepigrapha, Supplement Series 36 (London: Sheffield Academic, 2001), p. 123.

3. S. Dar, "Food and Archaeology in Romano-Byzantine Palestine," in *Food in An-

NOTES TO PAGES 45-52

tiquity, ed. J. Wilkens, D. Harvey, and E. Dobson (Exeter: University of Exeter Press, 1995), pp. 326-36, here p. 333.

4. C. Dauphin, "Plenty or Just Enough? The Diet of the Rural and Urban Masses of Byzantine Palestine," *Bulletin of the Anglo-Israel Archaeological Society* 17 (1999): 57.

5. S. Dar, *Landscape and Pattern: An Archaeological Survey of Samaria, 800 BCE–636 CE*, 2 vols. (Oxford: BAR, 1986).

6. Dar, "Food and Archaeology," p. 333.

7. B. Rosen, "Subsistence Economy of Stratum II," in *'Izbet Ṣarṭah*, ed. I. Finkelstein, BAR International 299 (Oxford: BAR, 1986), pp. 156-85.

8. Rosen, "Subsistence Economy of Stratum II."

9. B. Rosen, "Subsistence Economy in Iron Age I," in *From Nomadism to Monarchy: Archaeological and Historical Aspects of Ancient Israel*, ed. I. Finkelstein and N. Na'aman (Jerusalem: Israel Exploration Society, 1994), pp. 339-51.

10. Rosen, "Subsistence Economy in Iron Age I."

11. A. Sasson, "The Pastoral Component in the Economy of Hill Country Sites in the Intermediate Bronze and Iron Ages: Archaeo-Ethnographic Case Studies," *Tel Aviv* 25 (1998): 3-51.

12. Rosen, "Subsistence Economy in Iron Age I," pp. 347-49.

13. P. Halstead, "Plough and Power: The Economic and Social Significance of Cultivation with the Ox-Drawn Ard in the Mediterranean," *Bulletin of Sumerian Agriculture* 8 (1995): 11-22.

14. See, e.g., R. B. Coote and K. W. Whitelam, *The Emergence of Early Israel in Historical Perspective*, Social World of Biblical Antiquity 5 (Sheffield: Almond Press, 1987).

15. D. C. Hopkins, *The Highlands of Canaan: Agricultural Life in the Early Iron Age*, Social World of Biblical Antiquity 3 (Sheffield: JSOT Press, 1985).

Chapter 8: Environment and Climate

1. G. A. Smith, *The Historical Geography of the Holy Land* (London: Hodder and Stoughton, 1894).

2. For details see D. C. Hopkins, *The Highlands of Canaan: Agricultural Life in the Early Iron Age*, Social World of Biblical Antiquity 3 (Sheffield: JSOT Press, 1985), pp. 111-33; F. S. Frick, "Ecology, Agriculture and Patterns of Settlement," in *The World of Ancient Israel: Sociological, Anthropological, and Political Perspectives*, ed. R. E. Clements (Cambridge: Cambridge University Press, 1989), pp. 67-93; D. Baly, *The Geography of Palestine: A Study in Historical Geography* (London: Lutterworth, 1957).

3. See, for example, Hopkins, *The Highlands of Canaan*, pp. 72-75.

4. T. L. Thompson, *Early History of the Israelite People: From the Written and Archaeological Sources*, Studies in the History of the Ancient Near East 4 (Leiden: Brill, 1992), p. 234. See I. Finkelstein, "The Emergence of the Monarchy in Israel: The Environmental and Socio-Economic Aspects," *Journal for the Study of the Old Testament* 44 (1989): 43-74. In his account of subsistence economy in ancient Israel, Rosen pursues a

theoretical model for the Iron Age I village. His main model is a cereal-based agriculture (Izbet Sartah), but he also has another model of a herding village (Giloh) (B. Rosen, "Subsistence Economy in Iron Age I," in *From Nomadism to Monarchy: Archaeological and Historical Aspects of Ancient Israel*, ed. I. Finkelstein and N. Na'aman [Jerusalem: Israel Exploration Society, 1994], pp. 347-49).

5. See, for example, S. Dar, *Landscape and Pattern: An Archaeological Survey of Samaria, 800 BCE–636 CE*, 2 vols. (Oxford: BAR, 1986); Thompson, *Early History*, pp. 289-90. For a detailed description of the geomorphology of the Judean Hills and its implications for agriculture, see A. Ofer, "'All the Hill Country of Judah': From a Settlement Fringe to a Prosperous Monarchy," in *From Nomadism to Monarchy*, pp. 92-121.

6. Z. Herzog, "The Beer-Sheba Valley: From Nomadism to Monarchy," in *From Nomadism to Monarchy*, pp. 122-49, esp. pp. 124-26.

7. Baly, *The Geography of Palestine*; Hopkins, *The Highlands of Canaan*, pp. 99-108.

8. Herzog, "The Beer-Sheba Valley"; Thompson, *Early History of the Israelite People.*

9. Hopkins, *The Highlands of Canaan*, p. 84.

10. D. Sharon, "Variability of Rainfall in Israel: A Map of the Relative Standard Deviation of the Annual Amounts," *Israel Exploration Journal* 15 (1965): 169-76.

11. Hopkins, *The Highlands of Canaan*, p. 89. See also J. Neumann, "On the Incidence of Dry and Wet Years," *Israel Exploration Journal* 5 (1955): 137-53.

12. *b. Ta'anit* 19b. For third century A.D. concerns about rainfall in Palestine, see D. Sperber, "Drought, Famine and Pestilence in Amoraic Palestine," *Journal of the Economic and Social History of the Orient* 17 (1974): 272-98; R. Patai, "The 'Control of Rain' in Ancient Palestine," *Hebrew Union College Annual* 14 (1939): 251-86.

13. Frick, "Ecology," pp. 72-73.

14. This impression is easily given both with the translation "early rain and the later rain" (NRSV) and with "autumn rain and spring rain" (NIV).

15. Baly, *The Geography of Palestine*, p. 52.

16. D. Ashbel, "Israel, Land of (Geographical Survey): Climate," in *Encyclopaedia Judaica* (Jerusalem: Keter, 1971), 9:181-94, esp. p. 185.

17. C. Palmer, "Traditional Agriculture," in *The Archaeology of Jordan*, ed. B. MacDonald, R. Adams, and P. Bienkowski (Sheffield: Sheffield Academic, 2001), pp. 621-29.

Chapter 9: Food Shortage and Famine

1. Y. Aharoni, *The Land of the Bible: A Historical Geography*, 2nd ed. (London: Burns and Oates, 1979), p. 14.

2. See D. Sperber, "Drought, Famine and Pestilence in Amoraic Palestine," *Journal of the Economic and Social History of the Orient* 17 (1974): 272-98; R. Patai, "The 'Control of Rain' in Ancient Palestine," *Hebrew Union College Annual* 14 (1939): 251-86.

3. Josephus, *Antiquities* 15.299-316; 3.320-321; 20.51-53, 101 (cf. Acts 11:28).

4. Sperber, "Drought," p. 289.

5. F. M. Heichelheim, "Roman Syria," in *An Economic Survey of Ancient Rome,* ed. T. Frank (Baltimore: Johns Hopkins Press, 1938), pp. 121-257.

6. P. Garnsey, *Famine and Food Supply in the Graeco-Roman World: Response to Risk and Crisis* (Cambridge: Cambridge University Press, 1990).

7. P. Garnsey, "Famine in History," in *Understanding Catastrophe,* ed. J. Bourriau (Cambridge: Cambridge University Press, 1992), pp. 65-99, here pp. 69-70.

8. S. Dar, "Food and Archaeology in Romano-Byzantine Palestine," in *Food in Antiquity,* ed. J. Wilkens, D. Harvey, and E. Dobson (Exeter: University of Exeter Press, 1995), p. 333.

9. See D. C. Hopkins, *The Highlands of Canaan: Agricultural Life in the Early Iron Age,* Social World of Biblical Antiquity 3 (Sheffield: JSOT Press, 1985), pp. 211-61.

10. King and Stager make the rather perplexing observation that "this unusual mixture of foodstuffs, which is legally unclean (Lev. 19:19; Deut. 22:9) and may reflect a scarcity of food, is described as siege food" (P. J. King and L. Stager, *Life in Biblical Israel,* Library of Ancient Israel [Louisville: Westminster John Knox, 2001], p. 66). The uncleanness results from cooking over human dung as the exchange between God and Ezekiel makes clear (Ezek. 4:13-15).

11. Cf. P. Garnsey, *Food and Society in Classical Antiquity,* Key Themes in Ancient History (Cambridge: Cambridge University Press, 1999), pp. 37-41.

12. See, e.g., the recent collection of essays: F. Barker, P. Hulme, and M. Iversen, eds., *Cannibalism and the Colonial World* (Cambridge: Cambridge University Press, 1998).

Chapter 10: The Consumption of Meat: Archaeological Evidence

1. P. J. King, "Commensality in the Biblical World," in *Hesed Ve-Emet,* ed. E. S. Frerichs, J. Magness, and S. Gitin (Atlanta: Scholars, 1998), pp. 53-62, here p. 57; cf. "In biblical times meat was not a regular part of the diet" (J. F. Ross, "Food," in *The Interpreter's Dictionary of the Bible* [New York: Abingdon, 1962], 2:304-8, here p. 304).

2. S. Dar, "Food and Archaeology in Romano-Byzantine Palestine," in *Food in Antiquity,* ed. J. Wilkens, D. Harvey, and E. Dobson (Exeter: University of Exeter Press, 1995), p. 332.

3. A number of technical difficulties exist at this point, since the number of specimens can be counted in different ways. One approach is to give a raw account of the total bones counted for each species, the Number of Identified Specimens (NISP). If, for example, a fully articulated animal skeleton was discovered alongside a single mandible of another species, the NISP figure would suggest a picture at variance with the number of actual animals whose remains had been deposited and recovered at the site. Consequently archaeozoologists also calculate the Minimum Number of Individuals (MNI). The problem with this figure is that it may exaggerate the presence of rarer species. The MNI figure is considered more problematic, and archaeozoologists usually

cite the NISP for a species. For detailed discussion see S. Davis, *The Archaeology of Animals* (London: Batsford, 1987), pp. 34-35.

4. Two main methods for aging animal bones exist. The first method uses bone fusion. Fusion of long bones takes place at an age that is more or less constant within a species, allowing the proportion of adults and juveniles to be calculated. Since various bones fuse at different ages, it is possible to compile a kill-off profile. The problem with this method is that it tends to underestimate the number of mature animals. The second method is to examine tooth wear, although this tends to omit very young animals. For discussion of the different methods, see Davis, *The Archaeology of Animals*, pp. 39-44.

5. "In Europe and the Near East, the bane of most zooarchaeologists' lives is the distinction between sheep and goat bones and teeth" (Davis, *The Archaeology of Animals*, pp. 32-33). The proportion of sheep to goats is usually calculated by examination of the metacarpals. For discussion see Davis, pp. 32-34.

6. Sheep provide milk for three months a year, while goats provide for five months. The milk output for a sheep per year is about 40 liters, but for a goat is 70 liters (C. Palmer, "'Following the Plough': The Agricultural Environment of Northern Jordan," *Levant* 30 [1998]: 129-65).

7. S. Payne, "Kill-Off Patterns in Sheep and Goats: The Mandibles from Asvan Kale," *Anatolian Studies* 23 (1983): 281-301.

8. R. W. Redding, "Theoretical Determinants of a Herder's Decisions: Modeling Variation in the Sheep/Goat Ratio," in *Animals and Archaeology: 3. Early Herders and Their Flocks*, ed. J. Clutton-Brock and C. Grigson (Oxford: BAR, 1984), pp. 223-41. Redding showed that although it might be expected that a herder concentrate on either sheep or goats depending on whether dairy, fiber, or meat was being pursued, herders actually spread the risk by herding sheep and goats. In the light of the different reproductive levels of sheep and goats, a sheep/goat ratio of between 1:1 and 1.7:1 might be expected.

9. R. Cribb, "Computer Simulation of Herding Strategies as an Interpretive and Heuristic Device in the Study of Kill-Off Strategies," in *Animals and Archaeology*, pp. 161-70.

10. R. Cribb, "The Analysis of Ancient Herding Systems: An Application of Computer Simulation in Faunal Studies," in *Beyond Domestication in Prehistoric Europe*, ed. G. Barker and C. Gamble (New York: Academic Press, 1985), pp. 75-106.

11. P. Wapnish and B. Hesse, "Urbanization and the Organization of Animal Production at Tell Jemmeh in the Middle Bronze Age Levant," *Journal of Near Eastern Studies* 47 (1988): 81-94; P. Wapnish, "Archaeozoology: The Integration of Faunal Data with Biblical Archaeology," in *Biblical Archaeology Today, 1990: Proceedings of the Second International Congress on Biblical Archaeology*, ed. A. Biran and J. Aviram (Jerusalem: Israel Exploration Society, 1993), pp. 426-42. For a development of this within a Mesopotamian context, see M. A. Zeder, *Feeding Cities: Specialized Animal Economy in the Ancient Near East* (Washington, D.C.: Smithsonian Institution Press, 1991).

12. The contribution is often assessed by archaeozoologists by comparing the

overall weight of cattle bones to the weight of caprovine bones, since bone weight is a good indicator of meat provision.

13. P. Wapnish and B. Hesse, "Pig Use and Abuse in the Ancient Levant: Ethnoreligious Boundary-Building with Swine," in *Ancestors for the Pigs: Pigs in Prehistory,* ed. S. M. Nelson, MASCA Research Papers in Science and Archaeology (Philadelphia: University of Philadelphia Museum of Archaeology and Anthropology, 1998), pp. 123-36.

14. Hesse and Wapnish have produced a convenient and comprehensive table of significant mammal finds at Levantine sites from Pre-Pottery Neolithic B through to the Roman period. The number of identified specimens and the number of identifications per species are tabulated (B. Hesse and P. Wapnish, "An Archaeozoological Perspective on the Cultural Use of Mammals in the Levant," in *A History of the Animal World in the Ancient Near East,* ed. B. J. Collins [Leiden: Brill, 2001], pp. 457-91).

15. L. K. Horwitz and I. Milevski, "The Faunal Evidence for Socioeconomic Change between the Middle and Late Bronze Age in the Southern Levant," in *Studies in the Archaeology of Israel and Neighbouring Lands: In Memory of Douglas L. Esse,* ed. S. R. Wolff, ASOR Books 5 (Chicago: Oriental Institute of the University of Chicago; Atlanta: American Schools of Oriental Research, 2001), pp. 283-305.

16. J. Lev-Tov, "Pigs, Philistines, and the Ancient Animal Economy of Ekron from the Late Bronze Age to the Iron Age II" (Ph.D. diss., University of Tennessee, 2000).

17. Horwitz and Milevski observe in their conclusion that "there is, however, little faunal evidence to support a widespread return to pastoralism. The animal remains from sites in the hill country (Shiloh and Manaḥat), with the exception of the extremely high frequency of caprines at Shiloh, do not deviate from the general pattern of animal exploitation observed at the other LB sites" (Horwitz and Milevski, "Faunal Evidence," p. 301). The first part of this conclusion is true (though mainly because they are already predominantly pastoral economies), but the second part is difficult to justify from the evidence. Shiloh shows an increase in caprovines from 85 to 89 percent, with cattle decreasing from 12 to 9 percent (S. Hellwing, M. Sadeh, and V. Kishon, "Faunal Remains," in *Shiloh: The Archaeology of a Biblical Site,* ed. I. Finkelstein [Tel Aviv: Tel Aviv University, 1993], pp. 309-50). Manaḥat is more difficult to analyze because some of the material is from fills with animal bones from a variety of periods. Nevertheless, bones assigned to Middle Bronze IIB show 83 percent caprovines and 8 percent cattle, while Late Bronze has 82.5 percent caprovines and 10 percent cattle (L. K. Horwitz, "The Faunal Remains," in *Villages, Terraces, and Stone Mounds: Excavations at Manaḥat, Jerusalem, 1987-1989,* ed. G. Edelstein, I. Milevski, and S. Aurant, Israel Antiquities Authority Reports [Jerusalem: Israel Antiquities Authority, 1998], pp. 104-12). Thus, both Shiloh and Manaḥat have different characteristics from the other sites examined by Horwitz and Milevski (Dan, Tel Michal, Lachish, and Tell Jemmeh) and do not exhibit the agricultural intensification witnessed elsewhere.

18. The exception is Tel Masos in the Negev where 26.1 percent of the bones were from cattle (E. Tchernov and A. Drori, "Economic Patterns and Environmental Conditions at Hirbet El-Msas during the Early Iron Age," in *Ergebnisse der Ausgrabungen auf*

der Ḥirbet El-Mšaš [Ṭēl Māśoś] 1972-1975, ed. V. Fritz and A. Kempinski [Wiesbaden: Otto Harrassowitz, 1983], pp. 213-22). Tchernov and Drori argue that "the existence of the fallow deer *(D. dama mesopotamica)* and the intensive growth of cattle in Iron Age I indicates a climate more humid than the present one." There are conflicting opinions about the nature of the climate during Iron Age I, and there are dangers in claiming that anomalous animal patterns reflect climatic changes. For warnings about this see Wapnish, "Archaeozoology," pp. 426-30. Hesse and Wapnish, "An Archaeozoological Perspective on the Cultural Use of Mammals in the Levant," on the other hand, question whether these patterns of animal remains might not be the result of poor excavation techniques, possibly lack of sieving.

19. L. K. Horwitz, "Faunal Remains from Areas A, B, D, H and K," in *Excavations at the City of David, 1978-1985,* vol. 4, *Various Reports,* ed. D. T. Ariel and A. de Groot, Qedem 35 (Jerusalem: Hebrew University, 1996), pp. 302-17; B. Hesse, "Animal Bone Analysis," in *An Early Iron Age Village at Khirbet Raddana: The Excavations of Joseph A. Callaway,* ed. Z. Lederman (Ph.D. diss., Harvard University, 1999), pp. 103-18. "In this [Levantine] agricultural system, whenever the bovines amount to less than 5-7% of the ruminants, the economy of the society tends to be based mainly on sheep or goat herding. Whenever the percentage of bovines is 20% or more of the total ruminants, agriculture based on bovine-drawn ploughs seems to be the mainstay of the subsistence economy" (B. Rosen, "Subsistence Economy of Stratum II," in *'Izbet Ṣarṭah,* ed. I. Finkelstein, BAR International 299 [Oxford: BAR, 1986], pp. 156-85).

20. Hellwing, Sadeh, and Kishon, "Faunal Remains"; L. K. Horwitz, "Faunal Remains from the Early Iron Age Site on Mount Ebal," *Tel Aviv* 13-14 (1986): 173-89.

21. There is a preference for goats at Jerusalem (Horwitz, "Faunal Remains from Areas A, B, D, H and K"), Raddana (Hesse, "Animal Bone Analysis"), and Ebal (Horwitz, "Faunal Remains from the Early Iron Age Site on Mount Ebal"). Sites with almost equal levels of sheep and goats include Ai (Hesse, "Animal Bone Analysis"), Beth Shemesh (Hesse and Wapnish, "An Archaeozoological Perspective on the Cultural Use of Mammals in the Levant"), Lachish (P. Croft, "Archaeozoological Studies. Section A: The Osteological Remains [Mammalian and Avian]," in *The Renewed Archaeological Excavations at Lachish [1973-1994],* vol. 5, ed. D. Ussishkin [Tel Aviv: Tel Aviv University, 2004], pp. 2254-2348), and Tell Qiri (S. Davis, "The Faunal Remains," in *Tell Qiri: A Village in the Jezreel Valley,* ed. A. Ben-Tor and Y. Portugali, Qedem 24 [Jerusalem: Hebrew University, 1987], pp. 249-51).

22. Hesse, "Animal Bone Analysis."

23. S. Hellwing and Y. Adjeman, "Animal Bones," in *'Izbet Ṣarṭah,* pp. 141-52; E. F. Maher, "Iron Age Fauna from Tel Harasim Excavation 1996," in *The Eigth [sic] Season of Excavation at Tel Harrasim (Nahal Barkai), 1997,* ed. S. Givon (Tel Aviv: Bar Ilan University, 1998), pp. 13*-25*.

24. Rosen, "Subsistence Economy of Stratum II." In his study of 'Izbet Sartah, Sasson concludes, "the pastoralist component of the economy of 'Izbet Ṣarṭah was relatively small. The excess grain apparently was the basis of the economy of the village" (A. Sasson, "The Pastoral Component in the Economy of Hill Country Sites in the In-

termediate Bronze and Iron Ages: Archaeo-Ethnographic Case Studies," *Tel Aviv* 25 [1998]: 3-51).

25. E.g., "This [distribution of pigs at a site] may be the most valuable tool for the study of ethnicity of a given, single Iron I site" (I. Finkelstein, "Ethnicity and Origin of the Iron I Settlers in the Highlands of Canaan: Can the Real Israel Stand Up?" *Biblical Archaeology* 59 [1996]: 198-212, here p. 206).

26. Zeder observes that "pigs *(Sus scrofa)* are arguably the least well understood but most intriguing component of ancient Near Eastern animal economies" (M. A. Zeder, "Pigs and Emergent Complexity in the Ancient Near East," in *Ancestors for the Pigs: Pigs in Prehistory,* ed. S. M. Nelson [Philadelphia: University of Philadelphia Museum of Archaeology and Anthropology, 1998], pp. 109-22, here p. 109). Hesse and Wapnish outline a number of "pig principles" that are factors in the presence or absence of pig husbandry: pigs need more water than other stock; pigs are difficult to herd; pigs eat waste but are destructive of crops; they breed quickly and are a possible initial strategy for immigrant populations; they suit nonintensive agriculture; they have no secondary products; they suit urban populations desiring economic independence; they are associated with the lower classes; and certain texts associate them with particular rituals (Wapnish and Hesse, "Pig Use and Abuse in the Ancient Levant").

27. For discussion of the animal economy at Ekron, especially in relation to pig consumption and the Philistines, see Lev-Tov, "Pigs, Philistines, and the Ancient Animal Economy of Ekron from the Late Bronze Age to the Iron Age II," and summary in J. Lev-Tov, "The Social Implications of Subsistence Analysis of Faunal Remains from Tel Miqne-Ekron," *ASOR Newsletter* 49 (1999): 13-15.

28. S. Davis, "The Large Mammal Bones," in *Excavations at Tell Qasile: Part Two; The Philistine Sanctuary; Various Finds, the Pottery, Conclusions, Appendixes,* ed. A. Mazar, Qedem 20 (Jerusalem: Hebrew University of Jerusalem, 1985), pp. 148-50. Data for Tell Jemmeh published in Hesse and Wapnish, "An Archaeozoological Perspective on the Cultural Use of Mammals in the Levant," and taken from a paper by Wapnish, "Archaeozoology at Tell Jemmeh: Taphonomy and Paleoeconomy in Historic Archaeology" (unpublished paper presented to the National Geographic Society, 1985).

29. There is a move toward equal herd sizes in strata VI and VII before being reversed in Iron Age II (Lev-Tov, "Pigs, Philistines, and the Ancient Animal Economy of Ekron from the Late Bronze Age to the Iron Age II").

30. Lev-Tov, "Pigs, Philistines, and the Ancient Animal Economy of Ekron from the Late Bronze Age to the Iron Age II."

31. See Wapnish, "Archaeozoology at Tell Jemmeh."

32. Jerusalem (Horwitz, "Faunal Remains from Areas A, B, D, H and K") and Shiloh (Hellwing, Sadeh, and Kishon, "Faunal Remains") also show an increase.

33. Beersheba (S. Hellwing, "Human Exploitation of Animal Resources in the Early Iron Age Strata at Tel Beer-Sheba," in *Beer-Sheba I: Excavations at Tel Beer-Sheba, 1969-1971 Seasons,* ed. Y. Aharoni [Tel Aviv: Tel Aviv University Institute of Archaeology, 1973], pp. 105-15), Tel Ira (T. Dayan, "Faunal Remains: §1. Areas A-G," in *Tel 'Ira: A Stronghold in the Biblical Negev,* ed. I. Beit-Arieh [Tel Aviv: Tel Aviv University, 1999],

pp. 480-87; L. K. Horwitz, "Faunal Remains: §2. Areas L and M," in *Tel 'Ira,* pp. 488-94) and Tel Masos (Tchernov and Drori, "Economic Patterns and Environmental Conditions at Hirbet El-Msas during the Early Iron Age").

The slight increase in the number of animals killed before maturity in strata VII-VI at Beersheba (from 6.3 percent to 8.8 percent) does not justify Hellwing's conclusion that "it may be assumed that sheep, goats and cattle were exploited primarily for their meat rather than for other by-products, such as milk, wool or hides" (Hellwing, "Human Exploitation," p. 107). Such figures point to the importance of secondary products.

34. Lev-Tov, "Pigs, Philistines, and the Ancient Animal Economy of Ekron from the Late Bronze Age to the Iron Age II"; Hesse and Wapnish, "An Archaeozoological Perspective on the Cultural Use of Mammals in the Levant."

35. Data for Tel Hamid published in Hesse and Wapnish, "An Archaeozoological Perspective on the Cultural Use of Mammals in the Levant," and taken from T. Griffith and B. Hesse, "Preliminary Report on the Fauna from Tel Hamid" (unpublished paper presented to the Israel Antiquities Authority, 1999); D. R. Lipovitch, "Can These Bones Live Again? An Analysis of the Non-Canid, Mammalian Faunal Remains from the Achaemenid Period Occupation of Tel Ashkelon, Israel" (Ph.D. diss., Harvard University, 1999).

36. Lipovitch does not provide a reason for the low level of cattle at Ashkelon (Lipovitch, "Can These Bones Live Again?"). There is no obvious environmental explanation since at Early Bronze I Afridar, two kilometers north of Tel Ashkelon, there was an average of 22.1 percent cattle (S. W. Kansa, "Animal Exploitation at Early Bronze Age Ashqelon, Afridar: What the Bones Tell Us — Initial Analysis of the Animal Bones from Areas E, F and G," *Atiqot* 45 [2004]: 279-97).

37. Wapnish, "Archaeozoology."

38. The comparison of these three sites is subject to the obvious difficulties that stem from different collection and publication procedures and the size of samples. Davis's discussion of the animal remains from Tell Qiri does not distinguish between Iron Age strata. On the other hand, only six animal bones were recovered from Iron Age I strata at Tel Qashish, and consequently we have to rely on the 199 samples from Iron Age II. Note, however, Ben-Tor's observation that "sites such as Tel Qiri, about 2 km (1 mi.) south of Jokneam, and Tel Qashish, some 2 km to its north, were undoubtedly satellite settlements linked to the major city of Jokneam. The region thus provides an opportunity to investigate the material cultural aspect of the relationship between city and its satellite towns" (A. Ben-Tor, "Jokneam," in *The New Encyclopaedia of Archaeological Excavations in the Holy Land,* ed. E. Stern [New York: Simon and Schuster, 1993], pp. 805-11, here p. 805).

39. Davis, "The Faunal Remains." Y. Portugali discusses Tell Qiri's environment and possible land use in Y. Portugali, "Construction Methods, Architectural Features and Environment," in *Tell Qiri,* pp. 132-38.

40. L. K. Horwitz et al., "Faunal and Malacological Remains from the Middle Bronze, Late Bronze and Iron Age Levels at Tel Yoqne'am."

41. L. K. Horwitz, "Fauna from Tel Qashish," in *Tel Qashish: A Village in the Jezreel Valley; Final Report of the Archaeological Excavations (1978-1987)*, ed. A. Ben-Tor, R. Bonfil, and S. Zuckerman, Qedem Reports 5 (Jerusalem: Hebrew University, 2003), pp. 427-43.

42. There is also a drop in the percentage of bones that come from meat-rich limbs in Iron Age IIB.

43. L. K. Horwitz, "Animal Exploitation — Archaeozoological Analysis," in *Horbat Rosh Zayit: An Iron Age Storage Fort and Village*, ed. Z. Gal and Y. Alexandre, Israel Antiquities Authority Reports 9 (Jerusalem: Israel Antiquities Authority, 2000), pp. 221-32; R. Ziegler and J. Boessneck, "Tierrest der Eisenzeit II," in *Kinneret: Ergebnisse der Ausgrabungen auf dem Tell El-'Ormeam, See Gennesaret 1982-1985*, ed. V. Fritz (Wiesbaden: Harrassowitz, 1990), pp. 133-58; P. Wapnish and B. Hesse, "Faunal Remains from Tel Dan: Perspectives on Animal Production at a Village, Urban and Ritual Center," *Archaeozoologia* 4 (1991): 9-87.

44. L. K. Horwitz, "Mammalian Remains from Areas H, L, P, and Q," in *Excavations at Beth-Shean, 1989-1996*, vol. 1, *From the Late Bronze Age IIb to the Medieval Period*, ed. A. Mazar (Jerusalem: Israel Exploration Society, 2006), pp. 689-710. In a layer attributed to Assyrian destruction, a high percentage of pig remains was discovered (7 percent). Although the figure is unparalleled in any other Israelite site, the figures should be viewed with caution. The destruction layer provided only eighty-three bones, and thus the significance of the high pig figure is statistically questionable.

45. B. Hesse, "Fauna," in *Tel Madaba Archaeological Project, 1996, Preliminary Report*; http://www.utoronto.ca/tmap/prelim_1996.html (accessed 20 August 2007); Anon, "Fauna," in *Tel Madaba Archaeological Project, 1998-2000, Preliminary Report*; http://www.utoronto.ca/tmap/prelim_1998-2000.html (accessed 20 August 2007); D. West et al., *Analysis of Faunal Remains Recovered from Tell Nimrin, Dead Sea Valley, Jordan*; http://www.cwru.edu/affil/nimrin/stdy/adaj/osteo/2000_0.pdf (accessed 20 August 2007); P. Bienkowski, "The Animal Bones," in *Busayra: Excavations by Crystal-M. Bennett, 1971-1980*, ed. P. Bienkowski, British Academy Monographs in Archaeology 13 (Oxford: Oxford University Press, 2002), pp. 471-74; I. Köhler-Rollefson, "The Animal Bones," in *Excavations at Tawilan in Southern Jordan*, ed. C.-M. Bennett and P. Bienkowski, British Academy Monographs in Archaeology 8 (Oxford: Oxford University Press, 1995), pp. 97-100.

46. For the suggestion that cattle herding was found in Transjordan, see O. S. LaBianca and A. von den Driesch, eds., *Faunal Remains: Taphonomical and Zooarchaeological Studies of the Animal Remains from Tel Hesban and Vicinity*, Hesban 13 (Berrien Springs, Mich.: Andrews University Press, 1995), and O. S. LaBianca, *Sedentarization and Nomadization: Food System Cycles at Hesban and Vicinity in Transjordan*, Hesban 1 (Berrien Springs, Mich.: Andrews University Press, 1990), pp. 145-46. This is one of the few occasions in which archaeozoologists appeal to cattle herding as an explanation of faunal remains; cf. Dever's explanation of the high cattle figures at Tel Masos in the Iron Age (W. G. Dever, "How to Tell a Canaanite from an Israelite," in *The Rise of Ancient Israel*, ed. H. Shanks et al. [Washington, D.C.: Biblical Ar-

chaeological Society, 1992], pp. 26-56, esp. p. 48). LaBianca does not justify his appeal to cattle herding to explain the high level of cattle at Hesban: "A proposal that might account for this phenomenon is that during the Iron Age centuries, a fundamental shift took place in Transjordan in how cattle were utilized. Thus, whereas in the early Iron Age centuries cattle were raised, along with sheep and goats, as pasture animals, by Iron II Times this role was largely superseded by their role as draft animals" (p. 146). It is worth wondering whether those biblical texts that speak about the cattle of northern Transjordan have also influenced LaBianca's thinking (e.g., Num. 32:1; Amos 4:1). A number of considerations tell against this interpretation. First, the Hebrew word *miqneh*, often translated "cattle" (Num. 32:1), covers both cows *and* caprovines (see Gen. 26:14). This was also the case for the word "cattle" in the English language, where it could be used for any livestock. In the modern period the term "cattle" is used primarily for bovines, and the traditional translation of *miqneh* as "cattle" in English Bibles is consequently misleading. Second, Amos 4:1 could just as well be understood as a reference to plow-based agriculture as to cattle herding. Third, even in the Roman Empire with its more developed economy and more stratified society, cattle were not bred for the table. K. D. White notes that "there is no evidence that livestock of any kind was deliberately reared for the table, except in the matter of delicacies such as sucking pig" (White, *Roman Farming: Aspects of Greek and Roman Life* [Ithaca, N.Y.: Cornell University Press, 1970], p. 277). In the light of this, LaBianca's and Dever's comments need to be reevaluated.

47. E.g., Jerusalem (Horwitz, "Faunal Remains from Areas A, B, D, H and K"), Horvat Eleq (L. K. Horwitz, "The Animal Economy of Ḥorvat 'Eleq," in *Ramat Hanadiv Excavations: Final Report of the 1984-1988 Seasons,* ed. Y. Hirschfeld [Jerusalem: Israel Exploration Society, 2000], pp. 511-27), Tel Qashish (Horwitz, "Fauna from Tel Qashish"), and Yoqne'am (L. K. Horwitz and E. Dahan, "Animal Husbandry Practices during the Historic Periods," in *Yoqne'am I: The Late Periods,* ed. A. Ben-Tor, M. Avissar, and Y. Portugali, Qedem Reports 3 [Jerusalem: Hebrew University, 1996], pp. 246-55). In each case fewer than a hundred bones have been identified for the Persian period.

48. Lipovitch, "Can These Bones Live Again?"

Chapter 11: The Consumption of Meat: Anthropological Evidence

1. J. Wellhausen, *Prolegomena to the History of Israel* (Edinburgh: Adam and Charles Black, 1885), p. 63.

2. Note the telltale reference to the "ancient Semites," which is unusual for Wellhausen in his *Prolegomena.* Smith and Wellhausen had a close friendship and an admiration for each other's work.

3. W. R. Smith, *Lectures on the Religion of the Semites: Their Fundamental Institutions,* 3rd ed. (London: A. & C. Black, 1927), pp. 222-23. Smith was able to draw upon

classical sources, as well as comparative data from African explorers, for this suggestion (p. 297).

4. Smith, *Religion of the Semites*, p. 222.

5. Smith, *Religion of the Semites*, p. 238.

6. Smith, *Religion of the Semites*, p. 346.

7. A. Abu-Rabia, *The Negev Bedouin and Livestock Rearing: Social, Economic, and Political Aspects*, Mediterranea (Oxford: Berg, 1994), pp. 107-27.

Chapter 12: Food Distribution

1. J. Goody, *Cooking, Cuisine, and Class: A Study in Comparative Sociology*, Themes in the Social Sciences (Cambridge: Cambridge University Press, 1982).

2. For the development of some of these ideas on an unprecedented scale, see N. K. Gottwald, *The Tribes of Yahweh: A Sociology of the Religion of Liberated Israel, 1250-1200 BCE* (Sheffield: Sheffield Academic, 1999 [1979]).

3. R. B. Coote and K. W. Whitelam, *The Emergence of Early Israel in Historical Perspective*, Social World of Biblical Antiquity 5 (Sheffield: Almond Press, 1987).

4. T. L. Thompson, *Early History of the Israelite People: From the Written and Archaeological Sources*, Studies in the History of the Ancient Near East 4 (Leiden: Brill, 1992).

5. Meyers notes that the cooking of meat is often a male activity, while women are often given the more time-consuming but less prestigious tasks of cooking cereals and vegetables (C. Meyers, *Discovering Eve: Ancient Israelite Women in Context* [New York: Oxford University Press, 1988], p. 146).

6. Schmitt notes the importance of temples and festivals in her discussion of distribution (E. Schmitt, *Das Essen in der Bibel: Literaturethnologische Aspkete des Alltäglichen*, Studien zur Kulturanthropologie 2 [Münster: Lit, 1994]).

7. "The sumptuous provision of beef and lamb, and young and tender animals as well, points to eating on a scale far beyond the means of the ordinary worker or farmer. . . . The excessive behaviour described here was its own condemnation" (F. I. Andersen and D. N. Freedman, *Amos*, Anchor Bible 24A [New York: Doubleday, 1989], pp. 562-63).

Chapter 13: Nutritional Deficiencies

1. R. Ellison, "Diet in Mesopotamia: The Evidence of the Barley Ration Texts (c. 3000-1400 B.C.)," *Iraq* 43 (1981): 35-45; Ellison, "Some Thoughts on the Diet of Mesopotamia from c. 3000-600 B.C.," *Iraq* 45 (1983): 146-50.

2. Ellison, "Some Thoughts," p. 149.

3. D. S. McLaren et al., "Fat-Soluble Vitamins," in *Human Nutrition and Dietetics*,

ed. J. S. Garrow and W. P. T. James (Edinburgh: Churchill Livingstone, 1993), pp. 208-38, here p. 212.

4. Ellison, "Some Thoughts," p. 149.

5. P. Garnsey, *Food and Society in Classical Antiquity,* Key Themes in Ancient History (Cambridge: Cambridge University Press, 1999), pp. 20-21.

6. L. Hallberg, B. Sandström, and P. J. Aggett, "Iron, Zinc and Other Trace Elements," in *Human Nutrition and Dietetics,* pp. 174-207, here p. 182.

7. A. S. Prasad, "Zinc," in *The Cambridge World History of Food,* ed. K. F. Kiple and K. C. Omelas (Cambridge: Cambridge University Press, 2000), 1:868-75; Hallberg, Sandström, and Aggett, "Iron," pp. 188-95.

8. For studies on diet in pastoralist economies, see M. A. Nathan, E. M. Fratkin, and E. A. Roth, "Sedentism and Child Health among Rendille Pastoralists of Northern Kenya," *Social Science and Medicine* 43 (1996): 503-15; Nathan, Fratkin, and Roth, "Pastoral Sedentarization and Its Effects on Children's Diet, Health and Growth among Rendille of Northern Kenya," *Human Ecology* 32 (2004): 531-59; M. J. Casimir, *Flocks and Food: A Biocultural Approach to the Study of Pastoral Foodways* (Cologne: Böhlau Verlag, 1991).

9. D. J. Ortner and G. Theobald, "Paleopathological Evidence of Malnutrition," in *The Cambridge World History of Food,* 1:34-44, here p. 35 (with enumeration omitted).

10. The reasons for this lacuna have been discussed by R. Kletter, "People without Burials? The Lack of Iron I Burials in the Central Highlands of Palestine," *Israel Exploration Journal* 52 (2002): 28-48, and A. Faust, "'Mortuary Practices, Society and Ideology': The Lack of Iron Age I Burials in the Highlands in Context," *Israel Exploration Journal* 54 (2004): 174-90.

11. There were some noticeable exceptions. In particular, a substantial number of skeletal remains were discovered at Tel Lachish and two studies were subsequently published (D. L. Risdon, "A Study of the Cranial and Other Human Remains from Palestine Excavated at Tell Duweir [Lachish] by the Wellcome-Marston Archaeological Expedition," *Biometrika* 31 [1939]: 99-166, and M. J. Geller, "Diet and Regimen in the Babylonian Diet," in *Food and Identity in the Ancient World,* ed. C. Grottanelli and L. Milano, History of the Ancient Near East Studies 9 [Padua: Sargon, 2004], pp. 217-42). Unfortunately these early studies are primarily concerned with cranial measurements and have few observations about pathology. Nevertheless, the Lachish skulls are held in the Natural History Museum in London, and it may yet be hoped that they be reexamined for evidence of cribra orbitalia and dental pathologies.

12. For a brief history of paleopathology, see A. C. Aufderheide and C. Rodriguez-Martin, *The Cambridge Encyclopaedia of Human Paleopathology* (Cambridge: Cambridge University Press, 1998), pp. 1-10.

13. For a discussion of these issues, see C. Roberts, "Palaeopathology and Archaeology: The Current State of Play," in *The Archaeology of Medicine,* ed. R. Arnott (Oxford: Archaeopress, 2002), pp. 1-20.

14. The remains were unearthed from a burial cave on the western slopes of Mount Zion. The date and location of the remains would strongly suggest these were

Judahite burials, as also do the other archaeological finds (B. Arensberg and Y. Rak, "Jewish Skeletal Remains from the Period of the Kings of Judaea," *Palestine Exploration Quarterly* 117 [1985]: 30-34).

15. P. L. Stuart-Macadam, "Nutritional Deficiency Diseases: A Survey of Scurvy, Rickets and Iron-Deficiency Anemia," in *Reconstruction of Life from the Skeleton*, ed. M. Y. Isçan and K. A. R. Kennedy (New York: Liss, 1989), pp. 201-22, here p. 217.

16. Stuart-Macadam, "Nutritional Deficiency Diseases," p. 212.

17. Stuart-Macadam, "Nutritional Deficiency Diseases." For a statement about the current state of knowledge, see Aufderheide and Rodriguez-Martin, *Human Palaeopathology*, pp. 348-51.

18. Stuart-Macadam, "Nutritional Deficiency Diseases," pp. 219-20; Garnsey, *Food and Society*, pp. 43-61; N. Scrimshaw, C. E. Taylor, and J. E. Gordon, *Interactions of Nutrition and Infection* (Geneva: World Health Organization, 1968). Stuart-Macadam concludes her article on nutritional deficiency diseases in the following manner. "It is true that nutrition is an important aspect of the relationship between a population and its environment. However, a comprehensive survey of scurvy, rickets, and iron-deficiency anemia illustrates the importance of other culturally and environmentally determined factors involved in this relationship. There are complex adaptations between the human body, its nutrient requirements, and its environment. It is vital to have an appreciation of these complexities in any consideration of a 'nutritional deficiency' disease" (p. 220).

19. For the Middle Bronze Age, Smith, Bar-Yosef, and Sillen note figures of 63 percent in adults and 100 percent in children (however, the sample for children was only four individuals), for the Roman-Byzantine period 65 percent in adults and 62 percent in children (P. Smith, O. Bar-Yosef, and A. Sillen, "Archaeological and Skeletal Evidence for Dietary Change during the Late Pleistocene/Early Holocene in the Levant," in *Palaeopathology at the Origins of Agriculture*, ed. M. N. Cohen and G. J. Armelagos [Orlando: Academic Press, 1984], pp. 101-36, esp. pp. 120-21). A recent examination of skeletal remains from Middle Bronze Age Jericho found an incidence of 23 percent in a sample of thirteen orbital bones (S. Blau, "An Analysis of Human Skeletal Remains from Two Middle Bronze Age Tombs from Jericho," *Palestine Exploration Quarterly* 138 [2006]: 13-26). There are numerous observations of it in the population of Roman and Byzantine Jerusalem (see B. Arensberg, M. S. Goldstein, and Y. Rak, "Observations on the Pathology of the Jewish Population in Israel [100 BC to 600 CE]," *Koroth* 9 [1985]: 73-83; D. Hewin, "The Human Remains from Site N, Jerusalem," in *Excavations by K. M. Kenyon in Jerusalem, 1961-1967*, vol. 4, *The Iron Age Cave Deposits on the South-East Hill and Isolated Burials and Cemeteries Elsewhere*, ed. I. Eshel and K. Prag [Oxford: Oxford University Press, 1995], pp. 259-64; N. Haas, "Anthropological Observations on the Skeletal Remains from Giv'at Ha-Mivtar," *Israel Exploration Journal* 20 [1970]: 38-59), and a high level of incidence at Meiron in Galilee (P. Smith, E. Bournemann, and J. Zias, "The Excavated Tomb: The Skeletal Remains," in *Excavations at Ancient Meiron, Upper Galilee, Israel, 1971-72, 1974-75, 1977*, ed. E. M. Meyers, J. F. Strange, and C. L. Meyers [Cambridge, Mass.: American Schools of Oriental Research, 1981], pp. 107-20).

At Roman Ein Gedi 66 percent of children and 15 percent of adults displayed cribra orbitalia (H. Nathan and H. Haas, "'Cribra Orbitalia': A Bone Condition of the Orbit of Unknown Nature," *Israel Journal of Medical Science* 2 [1966]: 171-91). On the other hand, Nagar and Torgeé note an incidence of only 10 percent at Hellenistic and early Roman Samaria, and total absence from a sample of twelve individuals from the Shephelah (Y. Nagar and H. Torgeé, "Biological Characteristics of Jewish Burial in the Hellenistic and Early Roman Periods," *Israel Exploration Journal* 53 [2003]: 164-71). Small sample sizes may well account for much of the variation in the figures.

20. Rak and Arensberg do not present statistics for carious teeth and antemortem tooth loss. These figures are from P. Smith and S. Tau, "Dental Pathology in the Period of the Roman Empire: A Comparison of Two Populations," *OSSA: International Journal of Skeletal Research* 5 (1979): 35-40. Smith and Tau compare dental pathology in a late Second Temple Jewish population to samples from the Iron Age and Byzantine periods. The Iron Age sample consists of the skeletal remains examined by Arensberg and Rak (P. Smith, personal conversation).

21. M. Giles, "The Crania," in *Lachish III: The Iron Age,* ed. O. Tufnell (London: Oxford University Press, 1953), pp. 405-9.

22. See Smith and Tau, "Dental Pathology in the Period of the Roman Empire"; Smith, Bar-Yosef, and Sillen, "Dietary Change," pp. 123-25; P. Smith and L. K. Horwitz, "Culture, Environment and Disease: Palaeo-Anthropological Findings for the Southern Levant," in *Digging for Pathogenes,* ed. C. L. Greenblatt (Rehovot, Israel: Balaban Publishers, 1998), pp. 201-39, esp. pp. 222-23.

23. P. Smith, "The Skeletal Biology and Palaeopathology of Early Bronze Age Populations in the Levant," in *L'urbanisation de la Palestine á l'âge du Bronze ancien: Bilan et perspectives des recherches actuelles,* ed. P. de Miroschedji, BAR International Series 527 (Oxford: BAR, 1989), pp. 297-313.

24. V. Eshed, S. Wish-Baratz, and I. Hershkovitz, "Human Skeletal Remains," in *Tel 'Ira: A Stronghold in the Biblical Negev,* ed. I. Beit-Arieh (Tel Aviv: Tel Aviv University, 1999), pp. 495-520.

25. Smith and Horwitz, "Culture, Environment and Disease."

26. P. Smith and B. Peretz, "Hypoplasia and Health Status: A Comparison of Two Lifestyles," *Human Evolution* 6 (1986): 535-44, here p. 535.

27. A. Disi, W. Henke, and J. Wahle, "Human Skeletal Remains," in *Tel El Mazar I: Cemetery A,* ed. K. Yassine (Amman: University of Jordan, 1984), pp. 135-95.

28. P. Smith, L. K. Horwitz, and J. Zias, "Human Remains from the Iron Age Cemeteries at Akhziv: Part I; The Built Tomb from the Southern Cemetery," *Rivista di Studi Fenici* 18 (1990): 137-50.

29. Smith, Bar-Yosef, and Sillen, "Dietary Change," p. 123.

30. For discussion of strontium-calcium ratios, see A. Sillen, "Dietary Reconstruction and Near Eastern Archaeology," *Expedition* 28 (1986): 16-22.

31. S. C. Bisel, "Nutritional Chemistry of the Human Bones," in *Excavations at Tel Michal, Israel,* ed. Z. Herzog, G. Rapp, and O. Negbi (Minneapolis: University of Minnesota Press, 1989), pp. 230-33, here p. 233.

32. See P. Smith, "An Approach to the Palaeodemographic Analysis of Human Skeletal Remains from Archaeological Sites," in *Biblical Archaeology Today, 1990: Proceedings of the Second International Congress on Biblical Archaeology,* ed. A. Biran and J. Aviram (Jerusalem: Israel Exploration Society, 1993), pp. 2-13; Smith and Horwitz, "Culture, Environment and Disease."

33. Eshed, Wish-Baratz, and Hershkovitz, "Human Skeletal Remains," p. 507.

34. "Life expectancy at Jebel Qaʻaqir [MB I] was highest of all sites studied, followed by En-Gedi, Jericho and Meron [Hellenistic-Roman period]. Life expectancy was shortest at the Iron Age sites of Achzib and Tel Mazar and the recent sites of Dor and Beersheba [Ottoman]" (Smith, "Palaeodemographic Analysis," p. 10; cf. Disi, Henke, and Wahle, "Human Skeletal Remains"; Smith, Horwitz, and Zias, "Human Remains from the Iron Age Cemeteries at Akhziv"). "Most adults from all the archaeological sites appear to die before 50 years of age. The Iron Age seems to be the lowest and the Hellenistic the highest, from the point of view of percentage of older adults" (Smith and Horwitz, "Culture, Environment and Disease," pp. 226-27). For Tel Michal, see M. Hogan and S. C. Bisel, "Human Skeletal Remains," in *Excavations at Tel Michal, Israel,* pp. 226-29. The population at Tel Michal exhibits an extremely poor demographic profile, which leads Hogan and Bisel to question whether the sample is biased (p. 226). The high mortality rate among infants and young children (over 35 percent of children under five) is also noted, with malnutrition and/or acute infection suggested as a possible cause.

35. B. Arensberg, "Human Remains," in *Tell Qiri: A Village in the Jezreel Valley,* ed. A. Ben-Tor and Y. Portugali, Qedem 24 (Jerusalem: Hebrew University, 1987), pp. 27-33, here p. 28.

36. Nagar and Torgeé, "Biological Characteristics of Jewish Burial in the Hellenistic and Early Roman Periods."

Chapter 15: Biblical Diets

1. For a history and perceptive analysis, see R. M. Griffith, *Born Again Bodies: Flesh and Spirit in American Christianity* (Berkeley: University of California Press, 2004).

2. D. Colbert, *What Would Jesus Eat? The Ultimate Program for Eating Well, Feeling Great, and Living Longer* (Nashville: Nelson, 2002); J. Rogers, *The Bible's Seven Secrets to Healthy Eating* (Wheaton, Ill.: Crossway, 2001); J. Rubin, *The Maker's Diet: The Forty-Day Health Experience That Will Change Your Life Forever* (Lake Mary, Fla.: Siloam, 2004); R. Russell, *What the Bible Says about Healthy Living: Three Principles That Will Change Your Diet and Improve Your Health,* 2nd ed. (Ventura, Calif.: Regal, 2006).

3. Russell, *Healthy Living,* p. 155.

4. Rubin, *The Maker's Diet,* pp. 15, 82, 94-98.

5. "The Maker has given me a program for vibrant health based on His Word and the best available science, in that order" (Rubin, *The Maker's Diet,* p. 3). "Although much has been discovered in modern nutritional research, from which we can greatly

benefit, God's Word provides timeless principles that can help clear up contradictions and confusion in this field of study" (Rogers, *Seven Secrets,* p. 17; cf. pp. 68, 109).

6. In 2006 the Federal Trade Commission charged Rubin's company, Garden of Life, with making "unsubstantiated claims that their supplements treated or cured a variety of ailments, ranging from colds to cancer, and also made false claims of clinical proof" ("Dietary Supplement Maker Garden of Life Settles FTC Charges: Claimed Clinical Studies Backed Primal Defense, RM-10, Living Multi, and FYI," http://www.ftc.gov/opa/2006/03/gardenoflife.shtm [accessed 27 September 2007]).

7. Russell, *Healthy Living,* p. 16.

8. Russell, *Healthy Living,* pp. 186-87; Rubin, *The Maker's Diet,* p. 151. In Isa. 7:15 the preposition *le* could be interpreted in a temporal sense, so NRSV: "He shall eat curds and honey by the time he knows how to refuse the evil and choose the good." On the other hand, a final sense "in order that" is possible. However, the influence of diet on the development of brain function is clearly not in view; rather food is a means by which the child first begins to learn to choose.

9. Colbert, *What Would Jesus Eat?* pp. 35, 75.

10. Colbert, *What Would Jesus Eat?* p. 9; Russell, *Healthy Living,* p. 29.

11. In the world of "biblical diets" D. I. Macht's discredited attempt to show that nonkosher meats had higher levels of "toxicity" still captures the imagination. Macht believed that toxicity to humans could be assessed by examining the effect juices from animal muscles had on the growth of the seedlings of *Lupinus albus!* (D. I. Macht, "An Experimental Pharmacological Appreciation of Leviticus 11 and Deuteronomy 14," *Bulletin of the History of Medicine* 27 [1953]: 444-50). For use of Macht, see Russell, *Healthy Living,* pp. 144-45.

12. "I believe that no food is spiritually unclean in itself (see Rom. 14:14); however, I believe that eating unclean meat and not being circumcised can result in health problems, many of them serious or even deadly" (Russell, *Healthy Living,* p. 24).

13. Colbert, *What Would Jesus Eat?* p. 70.

14. Colbert, *What Would Jesus Eat?* p. 79.

15. Colbert, *What Would Jesus Eat?* p. 77. The consumer of "biblical diet" books may find this somewhat confusing set alongside Rubin's contempt for soybeans.

16. Colbert, *What Would Jesus Eat?* p. 144.

17. Rogers, *Seven Secrets,* pp. 61-63, 159-60.

18. "History reveals that the healthiest people in the world were generally the most *primitive* people as well. . . . One people group stands out among the many primitive cultures studied by anthropologists, health professionals, and nutritional historians. . . . That group was the nation of Israel, the chosen people of God" (Rubin, *The Maker's Diet,* pp. 32-34).

19. "Board of Directors"; available at http://www.westonaprice.org/board.html (accessed 27 September 2007).

20. The fact that these books are published by laypeople for laypeople may suggest a protest against the perceived priorities of the ordained profession.

21. For a detailed discussion of food in the Old Testament, see N. MacDonald, *Not*

Bread Alone: The Uses of Food in the Old Testament (Oxford: Oxford University Press, 2008).

22. For an important attempt to read the Old Testament with agrarian eyes, see E. F. Davis, *Remembering the Land: Biblical Interpretation and Ecological Responsibility* (forthcoming). I am grateful to Prof. Davis for making her work available to me.

Bibliography

Abu-Rabia, A. *The Negev Bedouin and Livestock Rearing: Social, Economic, and Political Aspects.* Mediterranea. Oxford: Berg, 1994.

Aharoni, Y. *Arad Inscriptions.* Jerusalem: Israel Exploration Society, 1981.

————. *The Land of the Bible: A Historical Geography.* 2nd ed. London: Burns and Oates, 1979.

Andersen, F. I., and D. N. Freedman. *Amos.* Anchor Bible 24A. New York: Doubleday, 1989.

Anon. "Fauna." In *Tel Madaba Archaeological Project, 1998-2000, Preliminary Report.* http://www.utoronto.ca/tmap/prelim_1998-2000.html. Accessed 20 August 2007.

Arensberg, B. "Human Remains." In *Tell Qiri: A Village in the Jezreel Valley,* edited by A. Ben-Tor and Y. Portugali, pp. 27-33. Qedem 24. Jerusalem: Hebrew University, 1987.

Arensberg, B., M. S. Goldstein, and Y. Rak. "Observations on the Pathology of the Jewish Population in Israel (100 BC to 600 CE)." *Koroth* 9 (1985): 73-83.

Arensberg, B., and Y. Rak. "Jewish Skeletal Remains from the Period of the Kings of Judaea." *Palestine Exploration Quarterly* 117 (1985): 30-34.

Ashbel, D. "Israel, Land of (Geographical Survey): Climate." In *Encyclopaedia Judaica,* 9:181-94. 16 vols. Jerusalem: Keter, 1971.

Aufderheide, A. C., and C. Rodriguez-Martin. *The Cambridge Encyclopaedia of Human Paleopathology.* Cambridge: Cambridge University Press, 1998.

Ausloos, H. "'A Land Flowing with Milk and Honey': Indicative of a Deuteronomistic Redaction?" *Ephemerides theologicae lovanienses* 75 (1999): 297-314.

Baly, D. *The Geography of Palestine: A Study in Historical Geography.* London: Lutterworth, 1957.

Barker, F., P. Hulme, and M. Iversen, eds. *Cannibalism and the Colonial World.* Cambridge: Cambridge University Press, 1998.

Bartlett, J. R. *Jericho.* London: Lutterworth, 1982.

Ben-Tor, A. "Jokneam." In *The New Encyclopaedia of Archaeological Excavations in the Holy Land,* edited by E. Stern, 3:805-11. New York: Simon and Schuster, 1993.

Bienkowski, P. "The Animal Bones." In *Busayra: Excavations by Crystal-M. Bennett, 1971-1980,* edited by P. Bienkowski, pp. 471-74. British Academy Monographs in Archaeology 13. Oxford: Oxford University Press, 2002.

Bisel, S. C. "Nutritional Chemistry of the Human Bones." In *Excavations at Tel Michal, Israel,* edited by Z. Herzog, G. Rapp, and O. Negbi, pp. 230-33. Minneapolis: University of Minnesota Press, 1989.

Blau, S. "An Analysis of Human Skeletal Remains from Two Middle Bronze Age Tombs from Jericho." *Palestine Exploration Quarterly* 138 (2006): 13-26.

Blenkinsopp, J. *Isaiah 1–39.* Anchor Bible 19. New York: Doubleday, 2000.

Borowski, O. *Agriculture in Ancient Israel.* Winona Lake, Ind.: Eisenbrauns, 1987.

———. *Daily Life in Biblical Times.* Atlanta: SBL, 2003.

———. *Every Living Thing: Daily Use of Animals in Ancient Israel.* Walnut Creek, Calif.: AltaMira, 1998.

Bottéro, J. "The Cuisine of Ancient Mesopotamia." *Biblical Archaeologist* 48 (1985): 36-47.

———. "The Most Ancient Recipe of All." In *Food in Antiquity,* edited by J. Wilkens, D. Harvey, and M. Dobson, pp. 248-55. Exeter: University of Exeter Press, 1995.

———. *Textes Culinaires Mésopotamiens: Mesopotamian Culinary Texts.* Mesopotamian Civilizations 6. Winona Lake, Ind.: Eisenbrauns, 1995.

Broshi, M. "The Diet of Palestine in the Roman Period: Introductory Notes." In *Bread, Wine, Walls, and Scrolls,* edited by M. Broshi, pp. 121-43. Journal for the Study of the Pseudepigrapha, Supplement Series 36. London: Sheffield Academic, 2001.

———. "Wine in Ancient Palestine: Introductory Notes." In *Bread, Wine, Walls, and Scrolls,* edited by M. Broshi, pp. 144-72. Journal for the Study of the Pseudepigrapha, Supplement Series 36. London: Sheffield Academic, 2001.

Brothwell, D., and P. Brothwell. *Food in Antiquity: A Survey of the Diet of Early Peoples.* London: Thomas and Hudson, 1969.

Caquot, A. "חָלָב chālābh." In *Theological Dictionary of the Old Testament,* edited by G. J. Botterweck and H. Ringgren, 4:386-91. Grand Rapids: Eerdmans, 1980.

Casimir, M. J. *Flocks and Food: A Biocultural Approach to the Study of Pastoral Foodways.* Cologne: Böhlau Verlag, 1991.

Clements, R. E. *Exodus.* Cambridge Bible Commentary. Cambridge: Cambridge University Press, 1972.

Clutton-Brock, J. "The Primary Food Animals of the Jericho Tell from the Proto-Neolithic to the Byzantine Period." *Levant* 3 (1971): 41-55.

Colbert, D. *What Would Jesus Eat? The Ultimate Program for Eating Well, Feeling Great, and Living Longer.* Nashville: Nelson, 2002.

Coote, R. B., and K. W. Whitelam. *The Emergence of Early Israel in Historical Perspective.* Social World of Biblical Antiquity 5. Sheffield: Almond Press, 1987.

Cribb, R. "The Analysis of Ancient Herding Systems: An Application of Computer Simulation in Faunal Studies." In *Beyond Domestication in Prehistoric Europe,* edited by G. Barker and C. Gamble, pp. 75-106. New York: Academic Press, 1985.

———. "Computer Simulation of Herding Strategies as an Interpretive and Heuristic Device in the Study of Kill-Off Strategies." In *Animals and Archaeology: 3. Early Herders and Their Flocks,* edited by J. Clutton-Brock and C. Grigson, pp. 161-70. Oxford: BAR, 1984.

Croft, P. "Archaeozoological Studies. Section A: The Osteological Remains (Mammalian and Avian)." In *The Renewed Archaeological Excavations at Lachish (1973-1994),* vol. 5, edited by D. Ussishkin, pp. 2254-2348. Tel Aviv: Tel Aviv University, 2004.

Curtis, R. I. *Ancient Food Technology.* Technology and Change in History 5. Leiden: Brill, 2001.

Dalman, G. *Arbeit und Sitte in Palästina, II: Der Ackerbau.* 7 vols. Hildesheim: Georg Olms, 1964 [1932].

———. *Arbeit und Sitte in Palästina, III: Von der Ernte zum Mahl.* 7 vols. Hildesheim: Georg Olms, 1964 [1933].

———. *Arbeit und Sitte in Palästina, IV: Brot, Öl und Wein.* 7 vols. Hildesheim: Georg Olms, 1964 [1935].

———. *Arbeit und Sitte in Palästina, VI: Zeltleben, Vieh- und Milchwirtschaft, Jagd, Fischfang.* 7 vols. Hildesheim: Georg Olms, 1964 [1939].

Dar, S. "Food and Archaeology in Romano-Byzantine Palestine." In *Food in Antiquity,* edited by J. Wilkens, D. Harvey, and E. Dobson, pp. 326-36. Exeter: University of Exeter Press, 1995.

———. *Landscape and Pattern: An Archaeological Survey of Samaria, 800 BCE–636 CE.* 2 vols. Oxford: BAR, 1986.

Dauphin, C. "Plenty or Just Enough? The Diet of the Rural and Urban Masses of Byzantine Palestine." *Bulletin of the Anglo-Israel Archaeological Society* 17 (1999): 39-65.

Davies, E. W. *Numbers.* New Century Bible. London: Marshall Pickering, 1995.

Davis, E. F. *Remembering the Land: Biblical Interpretation and Ecological Responsibility.* Forthcoming.

Davis, S. *The Archaeology of Animals.* London: Batsford, 1987.

———. "The Faunal Remains." In *Tell Qiri: A Village in the Jezreel Valley,* edited by

A. Ben-Tor and Y. Portugali, pp. 249-51. Qedem 24. Jerusalem: Hebrew University, 1987.

———. "The Large Mammal Bones." In *Excavations at Tell Qasile: Part Two; The Philistine Sanctuary; Various Finds, the Pottery, Conclusions, Appendixes,* edited by A. Mazar, pp. 148-50. Qedem 20. Jerusalem: Hebrew University of Jerusalem, 1985.

Dayan, T. "Faunal Remains: §1. Areas A-G." In *Tel 'Ira: A Stronghold in the Biblical Negev,* edited by I. Beit-Arieh, pp. 480-87. Tel Aviv: Tel Aviv University, 1999.

Derrett, J. D. M. "Whatever Happened to the Land Flowing with Milk and Honey?" *Vigiliae Christianae* 38 (1984): 178-84.

Dever, W. G. "How to Tell a Canaanite from an Israelite." In *The Rise of Ancient Israel,* edited by H. Shanks, W. G. Dever, B. Halpern, and P. K. McCarter, pp. 26-56. Washington, D.C.: Biblical Archaeological Society, 1992.

Disi, A., W. Henke, and J. Wahle. "Human Skeletal Remains." In *Tel El Mazar I: Cemetery A,* edited by K. Yassine, pp. 135-95. Amman: University of Jordan, 1984.

Driesch, A. von den, and J. Boessneck. "Final Report on the Zooarchaeological Investigation of Animal Bone Finds from Tell Hesban, Jordan." In *Faunal Remains,* edited by O. S. LaBianca and A. von den Driesch, pp. 65-108. Hesban 13. Berrien Springs, Mich.: Andrews University Press, 1995.

Ellison, R. "Diet in Mesopotamia: The Evidence of the Barley Ration Texts (c. 3000-1400 B.C.)." *Iraq* 43 (1981): 35-45.

———. "Some Thoughts on the Diet of Mesopotamia from c. 3000-600 B.C." *Iraq* 45 (1983): 146-50.

Epstein, I. *The Babylonian Talmud: Seder Seder Nezikin — Aboth.* London: Soncino Press, 1935.

Eshed, V., S. Wish-Baratz, and I. Hershkovitz. "Human Skeletal Remains." In *Tel 'Ira: A Stronghold in the Biblical Negev,* edited by I. Beit-Arieh, pp. 495-520. Tel Aviv: Tel Aviv University, 1999.

Faust, A. "'Mortuary Practices, Society and Ideology': The Lack of Iron Age I Burials in the Highlands in Context." *Israel Exploration Journal* 54 (2004): 174-90.

Federal Trade Commission. "Dietary Supplement Maker Garden of Life Settles FTC Charges: Claimed Clinical Studies Backed Primal Defense, RM-10, Living Multi, and FYI." http://www.ftc.gov/opa/2006/03/gardenoflife.shtm. Accessed 27 September 2007.

Feliks, Y. "Jewish Agriculture in the Period of the Mishnah." In *Eretz Israel from the Destruction of the Second Temple to the Muslim Conquests,* edited by Z. Baras, pp. 419-41. Jerusalem: Yad Ben Zvi, 1982.

Finkelstein, I. "The Emergence of the Monarchy in Israel: The Environmental and Socio-Economic Aspects." *Journal for the Study of the Old Testament* 44 (1989): 43-74.

————. "Ethnicity and Origin of the Iron I Settlers in the Highlands of Canaan: Can the Real Israel Stand Up?" *Biblical Archaeology* 59 (1996): 198-212.

Firmage, E. B. "Zoology (Fauna)." In *Anchor Bible Dictionary,* 6:1109-67. New York: Doubleday, 1992.

Foxhall, L., and H. A. Forbes. "*Sitometreia:* The Role of Grain as a Staple Food in Classical Antiquity." *Chiron* 12 (1982): 41-90.

Frankel, R. "Ancient Oil Mills and Presses in the Land of Israel." In *History and Technology of Olive Oil in the Holy Land,* edited by E. Ayalon, pp. 19-89. Tel Aviv: Eretz Israel Museum, 1994.

————. *Wine and Oil Production in Antiquity in Israel and Other Mediterranean Countries.* JSOT/ASOR Monograph Series 10. Sheffield: Sheffield Academic, 1999.

Frayn, J. M. *Subsistence Farming in Roman Italy.* London: Centaur Press, 1979.

————. "Wild and Cultivated Plants: A Note on the Peasant Economy of Roman Italy." *Journal of Roman Studies* 65 (1975): 32-39.

Freund, Richard A. "The Land Which Bled Forth Its Bounty: An Exile Image of the Land of Israel." *Scandinavian Journal of Theology* 13 (1999): 284-97.

Frick, F. S. "Ecology, Agriculture and Patterns of Settlement." In *The World of Ancient Israel: Sociological, Anthropological, and Political Perspectives,* edited by R. E. Clements, pp. 67-93. Cambridge: Cambridge University Press, 1989.

————. "'Oil from Flinty Rock' (Deuteronomy 32:13): Olive Cultivation and Olive Oil Processing in the Hebrew Bible — a Socio-Materialist Perspective." In *Food and Drink in the Biblical Worlds,* edited by A. Brenner and J. W. van Henten, pp. 1-17. Semeia 86. Atlanta: Society of Biblical Literature, 1999.

Galil, J. "An Ancient Technique for Ripening Sycomore Fruit in East Mediterranean Countries." *Economic Botany* 22 (1966): 178-90.

Garnsey, P. *Famine and Food Supply in the Graeco-Roman World: Response to Risk and Crisis.* Cambridge: Cambridge University Press, 1990.

————. "Famine in History." In *Understanding Catastrophe,* edited by J. Bourriau, pp. 65-99. Cambridge: Cambridge University Press, 1992.

————. *Food and Society in Classical Antiquity.* Key Themes in Ancient History. Cambridge: Cambridge University Press, 1999.

Geller, M. J. "Diet and Regimen in the Babylonian Diet." In *Food and Identity in the Ancient World,* edited by C. Grottanelli and L. Milano, pp. 217-42. History of the Ancient Near East Studies 9. Padua: Sargon, 2004.

Giles, M. "The Crania." In *Lachish III: The Iron Age,* edited by O. Tufnell, pp. 405-9. London: Oxford University Press, 1953.

Goody, J. *Cooking, Cuisine, and Class: A Study in Comparative Sociology.* Themes in the Social Sciences. Cambridge: Cambridge University Press, 1982.

Goor, A. "The History of the Date through the Ages in the Holy Land." *Economic Botany* 21 (1967): 320-40.

————. "The History of the Pomegranate in the Holy Land." *Economic Botany* 21 (1967): 215-29.

Gottwald, N. K. *The Tribes of Yahweh: A Sociology of the Religion of Liberated Israel, 1250-1200 BCE*. Sheffield: Sheffield Academic, 1999 [1979].

Gray, G. B. *Numbers*. International Critical Commentary. Edinburgh: T. & T. Clark, 1912.

Griffith, R. M. *Born Again Bodies: Flesh and Spirit in American Christianity*. Berkeley: University of California Press, 2004.

Griffith, T., and B. Hesse. "Preliminary Report on the Fauna from Tel Hamid." Unpublished paper presented to the Israel Antiquities Authority, 1999.

Haas, N. "Anthropological Observations on the Skeletal Remains from Giv'at Ha-Mivtar." *Israel Exploration Journal* 20 (1970): 38-59.

Hallberg, L., B. Sandström, and P. J. Aggett. "Iron, Zinc and Other Trace Elements." In *Human Nutrition and Dietetics*, edited by J. S. Garrow and W. P. T. James, pp. 174-207. Edinburgh: Churchill Livingstone, 1993.

Halstead, P. "Plough and Power: The Economic and Social Significance of Cultivation with the Ox-Drawn Ard in the Mediterranean." *Bulletin of Sumerian Agriculture* 8 (1995): 11-22.

Heichelheim, F. M. "Roman Syria." In *An Economic Survey of Ancient Rome*, edited by T. Frank, pp. 121-257. Baltimore: Johns Hopkins Press, 1938.

Hellwing, S. "Human Exploitation of Animal Resources in the Early Iron Age Strata at Tel Beer-Sheba." In *Beer-Sheba I: Excavations at Tel Beer-Sheba, 1969-1971 Seasons*, edited by Y. Aharoni, pp. 105-15. Tel Aviv: Tel Aviv University Institute of Archaeology, 1973.

Hellwing, S., and Y. Adjeman. "Animal Bones." In *'Izbet Ṣarṭah*, edited by I. Finkelstein, pp. 141-52. Oxford: BAR, 1986.

Hellwing, S., M. Sadeh, and V. Kishon. "Faunal Remains." In *Shiloh: The Archaeology of a Biblical Site*, edited by I. Finkelstein, pp. 309-50. Tel Aviv: Tel Aviv University, 1993.

Herzog, Z. "The Beer-Sheba Valley: From Nomadism to Monarchy." In *From Nomadism to Monarchy: Archaeological and Historical Aspects of Ancient Israel*, edited by I. Finkelstein and N. Na'aman, pp. 122-49. Jerusalem: Israel Exploration Society, 1994.

Hesse, B. "Animal Bone Analysis." In "An Early Iron Age Village at Khirbet Raddana: The Excavations of Joseph A. Callaway," edited by Z. Lederman, pp. 103-18. Ph.D. diss., Harvard University, 1999.

————. "Fauna." In *Tel Madaba Archaeological Project, 1996, Preliminary Report*. http://www.utoronto.ca/tmap/prelim_1996.html. Accessed 20 August 2007.

Hesse, B., and P. Wapnish. "An Archaeozoological Perspective on the Cultural Use of Mammals in the Levant." In *A History of the Animal World in the Ancient Near East*, edited by B. J. Collins, pp. 457-91. Leiden: Brill, 2001.

Hewin, D. "The Human Remains from Site N, Jerusalem." In *Excavations by K. M. Kenyon in Jerusalem, 1961-1967,* vol. 4, *The Iron Age Cave Deposits on the South-East Hill and Isolated Burials and Cemeteries Elsewhere,* edited by I. Eshel and K. Prag, pp. 259-64. Oxford: Oxford University Press, 1995.

Hogan, M., and S. C. Bisel. "Human Skeletal Remains." In *Excavations at Tel Michal, Israel,* edited by Z. Herzog, G. Rapp, and O. Negbi, pp. 226-29. Minneapolis: University of Minnesota Press, 1989.

Hopkins, D. C. *The Highlands of Canaan: Agricultural Life in the Early Iron Age.* Social World of Biblical Antiquity 3. Sheffield: JSOT Press, 1985.

Horwitz, L. K. "The Animal Economy of Ḥorvat 'Eleq." In *Ramat Hanadiv Excavations: Final Report of the 1984-1988 Seasons,* edited by Y. Hirschfeld, pp. 511-27. Jerusalem: Israel Exploration Society, 2000.

———. "Animal Exploitation — Archaeozoological Analysis." In *Ḥorbat Rosh Zayit: An Iron Age Storage Fort and Village,* edited by Z. Gal and Y. Alexandre, pp. 221-32. Israel Antiquities Authority Reports 9. Jerusalem: Israel Antiquities Authority, 2000.

———. "Fauna from Tel Qashish." In *Tel Qashish: A Village in the Jezreel Valley; Final Report of the Archaeological Excavations (1978-1987),* edited by A. Ben-Tor, R. Bonfil, and S. Zuckerman, pp. 427-43. Qedem Reports 5. Jerusalem: Hebrew University, 2003.

———. "The Faunal Remains." In *Villages, Terraces, and Stone Mounds: Excavations at Manaḥat, Jerusalem, 1987-1989,* edited by G. Edelstein, I. Milevski, and S. Aurant, pp. 104-12. Israel Antiquities Authority Reports. Jerusalem: Israel Antiquities Authority, 1998.

———. "Faunal Remains: §2. Areas L and M." In *Tel 'Ira: A Stronghold in the Biblical Negev,* edited by I. Beit-Arieh, pp. 488-94. Tel Aviv: Tel Aviv University, 1999.

———. "Faunal Remains from Areas A, B, D, H and K." In *Excavations at the City of David, 1978-1985,* vol. 4, *Various Reports,* edited by D. T. Ariel and A. de Groot, pp. 302-17. Qedem 35. Jerusalem: Hebrew University, 1996.

———. "Faunal Remains from the Early Iron Age Site on Mount Ebal." *Tel Aviv* 13-14 (1986): 173-89.

———. "Mammalian Remains from Areas H, L, P, and Q." In *Excavations at Beth-Shean, 1989-1996,* vol. 1, *From the Late Bronze Age IIb to the Medieval Period,* edited by A. Mazar, pp. 689-710. Jerusalem: Israel Exploration Society, 2006.

Horwitz, L. K., N. Bar Giora, H. K. Mienis, and O. Lernau. "Faunal and Malacological Remains from the Middle Bronze, Late Bronze and Iron Age Levels at Tel Yoqne'am." In *Yoqne'am III: The Middle and Late Bronze Ages; Final Report of the Archaeological Excavations (1977-1988),* edited by A. Ben-Tor, D. Ben-Ami, and A. Livneh, pp. 395-435. Qedem 7. Jerusalem: Institute of Archaeology, Hebrew University of Jerusalem, 2005.

Horwitz, L. K., and E. Dahan. "Animal Husbandry Practices during the Historic Periods." In *Yoqne'am I: The Late Periods,* edited by A. Ben-Tor, M. Avissar, and Y. Portugali, pp. 246-55. Qedem Reports 3. Jerusalem: Hebrew University, 1996.

Horwitz, L. K., and I. Milevski. "The Faunal Evidence for Socioeconomic Change between the Middle and Late Bronze Age in the Southern Levant." In *Studies in the Archaeology of Israel and Neighbouring Lands: In Memory of Douglas L. Esse,* edited by S. R. Wolff, pp. 283-305. ASOR Books 5. Chicago: Oriental Institute of the University of Chicago; Atlanta: American Schools of Oriental Research, 2001.

Horwitz, L. K., and E. Tchernov. "Bird Remains from Areas A, D, H and K." In *Excavations at the City of David, 1978-1985,* vol. 4, *Various Reports,* edited by D. T. Ariel and A. de Groot, pp. 298-301. Qedem 35. Jerusalem: Hebrew University, 1996.

———. "Subsistence Patterns in Ancient Jerusalem: A Study of Animal Remains from the Ophel." In *Excavations in the South of the Temple Mount: The Ophel of Biblical Jerusalem,* edited by E. Mazar and B. Mazar, pp. 144-54. Qedem 29. Jerusalem: Hebrew University of Jerusalem, 1989.

Josephus, *The Jewish War, Books I-III.* Translated by H. St. J. Thackeray. London: William Heinemann, 1927.

Kansa, S. W. "Animal Exploitation at Early Bronze Age Ashqelon, Afridar: What the Bones Tell Us — Initial Analysis of the Animal Bones from Areas E, F and G." *Atiqot* 45 (2004): 279-97.

King, P. J. "Commensality in the Biblical World." In *Hesed Ve-Emet,* edited by E. S. Frerichs, J. Magness, and S. Gitin, pp. 53-62. Atlanta: Scholars, 1998.

King, P. J., and L. Stager. *Life in Biblical Israel.* Library of Ancient Israel. Louisville: Westminster John Knox, 2001.

Kislev, M. E. "The Identification of *Hitta* and *Kussemet.*" *Leshonenu* 37 (1973): 83-95, 243-52.

Kletter, R. "People without Burials? The Lack of Iron I Burials in the Central Highlands of Palestine." *Israel Exploration Journal* 52 (2002): 28-48.

Knipping, B. R. "Die Wortkombination 'Land, Fließend Milch und Honig': Eine kurze Problematisierung ihrer Ausdeutung, ihrer Überlieferungsgeschichte und der Tragweite eines Pentateuchmodells." *Biblische Notizen* 98 (1999): 55-71.

Köhler, L. "Jes 30,24 בליל חמיץ." *Zeitschrift für die alttestamentliche Wissenschaft* 40 (1922): 15-17.

Köhler-Rollefson, I. "The Animal Bones." In *Excavations at Tawilan in Southern Jordan,* edited by C.-M. Bennett and P. Bienkowski, pp. 97-100. British Academy Monographs in Archaeology 8. Oxford: Oxford University Press, 1995.

LaBianca, O. S. *Sedentarization and Nomadization: Food System Cycles at Hesban and Vicinity in Transjordan.* Hesban 1. Berrien Springs, Mich.: Andrews University Press, 1990.

LaBianca, O. S., and A. von den Driesch, eds. *Faunal Remains: Taphonomical and Zooarchaeological Studies of the Animal Remains from Tel Hesban and Vicinity.* Hesban 13. Berrien Springs, Mich.: Andrews University Press, 1995.

Lernau, H., and O. Lernau. "Fish Bone Remains." In *Excavations in the South of the Temple Mount: The Ophel of Biblical Jerusalem,* edited by E. Mazar and B. Mazar, pp. 155-61. Qedem 29. Jerusalem: Hebrew University, 1989.

————. "Fish Remains." In *Excavations at the City of David, 1978-1985: Stratigraphical, Environmental, and Other Reports,* edited by A. de Groot and D. T. Ariel, pp. 131-48. Qedem 33. Jerusalem: Hebrew University, 1992.

Lernau, O. "Fish Bones." In *Meggido III: The 1992-1996 Seasons,* vol. 2, edited by I. Finkelstein, D. Ussishkin, and B. Halpern, pp. 463-77. Tel Aviv: Tel Aviv University, 2000.

————. "Fish Bones." In *Tel Kabri: The 1986-1993 Excavation Seasons,* edited by A. Kempinski, pp. 409-27. Tel Aviv: Tel Aviv University, 2002.

————. "Fish Bones from Ḥorbat Rosh Zayit." In *Ḥorbat Rosh Zayit: An Iron Age Storage Fort and Village,* edited by Z. Gal and Y. Alexandre, pp. 233-37. Israel Antiquities Authority Reports. Jerusalem: Israel Antiquities Authority, 2000.

————. "Fish Remains at Tel Harassim." In *The Eleventh Season of Excavation at Tel Harassim (Nahal Barkai), 2000,* edited by S. Givon, pp. 4*-12*. Tel Aviv: Bar Ilan University, 2002.

————. "Fish Remains from Tel Harassim." In *The Sixth Season of Excavation at Tel Harassim (Nahal Barkai), 1995,* edited by S. Givon, pp. 14*-23*. Tel Aviv: Bar Ilan University, 1996.

Lernau, O., and D. Golani. "Section B: The Osteological Remains (Aquatic)." In *The Renewed Archaeological Excavations at Lachish (1973-1994),* vol. 5, edited by D. Ussishkin, pp. 2456-89. Tel Aviv: Tel Aviv University, 2004.

Levine, E. "The Land of Milk and Honey." *Journal for the Study of the Old Testament* 87 (2000): 43-57.

Lev-Tov, J. "Pigs, Philistines, and the Ancient Animal Economy of Ekron from the Late Bronze Age to the Iron Age II." Ph.D. diss., University of Tennessee, 2000.

————. "The Social Implications of Subsistence Analysis of Faunal Remains from Tel Miqne-Ekron." *ASOR Newsletter* 49 (1999): 13-15.

Lichtheim, M. *Ancient Egyptian Literature: A Book of Readings.* Vol. 1, *The Old and Middle Kingdoms.* Berkeley: University of California Press, 1973.

Lipovitch, D. R. "Can These Bones Live Again? An Analysis of the Non-Canid, Mammalian Faunal Remains from the Achaemenid Period Occupation of Tel Ashkelon, Israel." Ph.D. diss., Harvard University, 1999.

Lohfink, N. "'I Am Yahweh, Your Physician' (Exodus 15:26): God, Society and Human Health in a Postexilic Revision of the Pentateuch (Exod. 15:2b, 26)." In

Theology of the Pentateuch: Themes of the Priestly Narrative and Deuteronomy, pp. 35-95. Edinburgh: T. & T. Clark, 1994.

Löw, I. *Die Flora Der Juden.* 4 vols. Hildesheim: Georg Olms, 1967 [1924].

MacDonald, N. *Not Bread Alone: The Uses of Food in the Old Testament.* Oxford: Oxford University Press, 2008.

Macht, D. I. "An Experimental Pharmacological Appreciation of Leviticus 11 and Deuteronomy 14." *Bulletin of the History of Medicine* 27 (1953): 444-50.

Maher, E. F. "Iron Age Fauna from Tel Harasim Excavation 1996." In *The Eigth [sic] Season of Excavation at Tel Harassim (Nahal Barkai), 1997,* edited by S. Givon, pp. 13*-25*. Tel Aviv: Bar Ilan University, 1998.

Matthews, V. H. "Treading the Winepress: Actual and Metaphorical Viticulture in the Ancient Near East." In *Food and Drink in the Biblical Worlds,* edited by A. Brenner and J. W. van Henten, pp. 19-32. Semeia 86. Atlanta: Society of Biblical Literature, 1999.

Mayes, A. D. H. *Deuteronomy.* New Century Bible. London: Oliphants, 1979.

Mazar, A., *The Tel Rehov Excavations — 2007.* http://www.rehov.org/bee.htm. Accessed 10 October 2007.

McLaren, D. S., et al. "Fat-Soluble Vitamins." In *Human Nutrition and Dietetics,* edited by J. S. Garrow and W. P. T. James, pp. 208-38. Edinburgh: Churchill Livingstone, 1993.

Meyers, C. *Discovering Eve: Ancient Israelite Women in Context.* New York: Oxford University Press, 1988.

Milgrom, J. *Leviticus 1–16.* Anchor Bible 3. New York: Doubleday, 1991.

———. *Leviticus 23–27: A New Translation with Introduction and Commentary.* Anchor Bible 3B. New York: Doubleday, 2001.

Nagar, Y., and H. Torgeé. "Biological Characteristics of Jewish Burial in the Hellenistic and Early Roman Periods." *Israel Exploration Journal* 53 (2003): 164-71.

Nathan, H., and H. Haas. "'Cribra Orbitalia': A Bone Condition of the Orbit of Unknown Nature." *Israel Journal of Medical Science* 2 (1966): 171-91.

Nathan, M. A., E. M. Fratkin, and E. A. Roth. "Pastoral Sedentarization and Its Effects on Children's Diet, Health and Growth among Rendille of Northern Kenya." *Human Ecology* 32 (2004): 531-59.

———. "Sedentism and Child Health among Rendille Pastoralists of Northern Kenya." *Social Science and Medicine* 43 (1996): 503-15.

Naveh, J. "The Aramaic Ostraca from Tel Arad." In Y. Aharoni, *Arad Inscriptions,* pp. 153-76. Jerusalem: Israel Exploration Society, 1981.

Neef, R. "Plants." In *Picking Up the Threads: A Continuing Review of Excavations at Deir Alla, Jordan,* edited by G. van der Kooij and M. M. Ibrahim, pp. 30-37. Leiden: University of Leiden Archaeological Centre, 1989.

Neufeld, E. "Apiculture in Ancient Palestine (Early and Middle Iron Age) within the Framework of the Ancient Near East." *Ugarit-Forschungen* 10 (1978): 238-47.

Neumann, J. "On the Incidence of Dry and Wet Years." *Israel Exploration Journal* 5 (1955): 137-53.

Neusner, J. *Mishnah: A New Translation.* New Haven: Yale University Press, 1988.

———. *Torah from Our Sages: Pirke Avot.* Chappaqua, N.Y.: Rossel Books, 1983.

Ofer, A. "'All the Hill Country of Judah': From a Settlement Fringe to a Prosperous Monarchy." In *From Nomadism to Monarchy: Archaeological and Historical Aspects of Ancient Israel,* edited by I. Finkelstein and N. Na'aman, pp. 92-121. Jerusalem: Israel Exploration Society, 1994.

Origen. *On First Principles.* Translated by G. W. Butterworth. New York: Harper and Row, 1966.

Ortner, D. J., and G. Theobald. "Paleopathological Evidence of Malnutrition." In *The Cambridge World History of Food,* edited by K. F. Kiple and K. C. Ornelas, 1:34-44. Cambridge: Cambridge University Press, 2000.

Palmer, C. "'Following the Plough': The Agricultural Environment of Northern Jordan." *Levant* 30 (1998): 129-65.

———. "Milk and Cereals: Identifying Food and Food Identity among Fallāḥīn and Bedouin in Jordan." *Levant* 34 (2002): 173-95.

———. "Traditional Agriculture." In *The Archaeology of Jordan,* edited by B. MacDonald, R. Adams, and P. Bienkowski, pp. 621-29. Sheffield: Sheffield Academic, 2001.

Patai, R. "The 'Control of Rain' in Ancient Palestine." *Hebrew Union College Annual* 14 (1939): 251-86.

Payne, S. "Kill-Off Patterns in Sheep and Goats: The Mandibles from Asvan Kale." *Anatolian Studies* 23 (1983): 281-301.

Pope, M. *Job.* Anchor Bible 15. Garden City, N.Y.: Doubleday, 1965.

Portugali, Y. "Construction Methods, Architectural Features and Environment." In *Tell Qiri: A Village in the Jezreel Valley,* edited by A. Ben-Tor and Y. Portugali, pp. 132-38. Qedem 24. Jerusalem: Hebrew University, 1987.

Prasad, A. S. "Zinc." In *The Cambridge World History of Food,* edited by K. F. Kiple and K. C. Omelas, 1:868-75. Cambridge: Cambridge University Press, 2000.

Pritchard, J. B. *Winery, Defenses, and Soundings at Gibeon.* Philadelphia: Pennsylvania University Museum, 1964.

Rainey, A. F. "Three Additional Texts." In Y. Aharoni, *Arad Inscriptions,* pp. 122-25. Jerusalem: Israel Exploration Society, 1981.

Raphael, O., and O. Lernau. "Faunal Remains from Bab-El-Hawa: An Iron Age–Byzantine Site in the Golan Heights." *Archaeozoologia* 8 (1996): 105-18.

Redding, R. W. "Theoretical Determinants of a Herder's Decisions: Modeling Variation in the Sheep/Goat Ratio." In *Animals and Archaeology: 3. Early Herders and Their Flocks,* edited by J. Clutton-Brock and C. Grigson, pp. 223-41. Oxford: BAR, 1984.

Reisner, G. A., C. S. Fisher, and D. G. Lyon. *Harvard Excavations at Samaria, 1908-1910.* Vol. 1. Cambridge: Harvard University Press, 1924.

Renfrew, J. M. *Palaeoethnobotany: The Prehistoric Food Plants of the Near East and Europe.* London: Methuen, 1973.

Risdon, D. L. "A Study of the Cranial and Other Human Remains from Palestine Excavated at Tell Duweir (Lachish) by the Wellcome-Marston Archaeological Expedition." *Biometrika* 31 (1939): 99-166.

Roberts, C. "Palaeopathology and Archaeology: The Current State of Play." In *The Archaeology of Medicine,* edited by R. Arnott, pp. 1-20. Oxford: Archaeopress, 2002.

Rogers, J. *The Bible's Seven Secrets to Healthy Eating.* Wheaton, Ill.: Crossway, 2001.

Rosen, B. "Subsistence Economy in Iron Age I." In *From Nomadism to Monarchy: Archaeological and Historical Aspects of Ancient Israel,* edited by I. Finkelstein and N. Na'aman, pp. 339-51. Jerusalem: Israel Exploration Society, 1994.

———. "Subsistence Economy of Stratum II." In *'Izbet Ṣarṭah,* edited by I. Finkelstein, pp. 156-85. BAR International 299. Oxford: BAR, 1986.

———. "Wine and Oil Allocations in the Samaria Ostraca." *Tel Aviv* 13-14 (1986-87): 39-45.

Ross, J. F. "Food." In *The Interpreter's Dictionary of the Bible,* 2:304-8. New York: Abingdon, 1962.

Rubin, J. *The Maker's Diet: The Forty-Day Health Experience That Will Change Your Life Forever.* Lake Mary, Fla.: Siloam, 2004.

Russell, R. *What the Bible Says about Healthy Living: Three Principles That Will Change Your Diet and Improve Your Health.* 2nd ed. Ventura, Calif.: Regal, 2006.

Ryder, M. L. "Sheep and Goat Husbandry with Particular Reference to Textile Fibre and Milk Production." *Bulletin of Sumerian Agriculture* 7 (1993): 9-32.

Safrai, Z. *The Economy of Roman Palestine.* London: Routledge, 1994.

Sasson, A. "The Pastoral Component in the Economy of Hill Country Sites in the Intermediate Bronze and Iron Ages: Archaeo-Ethnographic Case Studies." *Tel Aviv* 25 (1998): 3-51.

Sasson, J. M. "The Blood of Grapes: Viticulture and Intoxication in the Hebrew Bible." In *Drinking in Ancient Societies: History and Culture of Drinks in the Ancient Near East,* edited by L. Milano, pp. 399-419. History of the Ancient Near East Studies 6. Padua: Sargon, 1994.

Schmitt, E. *Das Essen in der Bibel: Literaturethnologische Aspkete des Alltäglichen.* Studien zur Kulturanthropologie 2. Münster: Lit, 1994.

Scrimshaw, N., C. E. Taylor, and J. E. Gordon. *Interactions of Nutrition and Infection.* Geneva: World Health Organization, 1968.

Sharon, D. "Variability of Rainfall in Israel: A Map of the Relative Standard Deviation of the Annual Amounts." *Israel Exploration Journal* 15 (1965): 169-76.

Sillen, A. "Dietary Reconstruction and Near Eastern Archaeology." *Expedition* 28 (1986): 16-22.

Smith, G. A. *The Historical Geography of the Holy Land.* London: Hodder and Stoughton, 1894.

Smith, P. "An Approach to the Palaeodemographic Analysis of Human Skeletal Remains from Archaeological Sites." In *Biblical Archaeology Today, 1990: Proceedings of the Second International Congress on Biblical Archaeology,* edited by A. Biran and J. Aviram, pp. 2-13. Jerusalem: Israel Exploration Society, 1993.

————. "The Skeletal Biology and Palaeopathology of Early Bronze Age Populations in the Levant." In *L'urbanisation de la Palestine á l'âge du Bronze ancien: Bilan et perspectives des recherches actuelles,* edited by P. de Miroschedji, pp. 297-313. BAR International Series 527. Oxford: BAR, 1989.

Smith, P., O. Bar-Yosef, and A. Sillen. "Archaeological and Skeletal Evidence for Dietary Change during the Late Pleistocene/Early Holocene in the Levant." In *Palaeopathology at the Origins of Agriculture,* edited by M. N. Cohen and G. J. Armelagos, pp. 101-36. Orlando: Academic Press, 1984.

Smith, P., E. Bournemann, and J. Zias. "The Excavated Tomb: The Skeletal Remains." In *Excavations at Ancient Meiron, Upper Galilee, Israel, 1971-72, 1974-75, 1977,* edited by E. M. Meyers, J. F. Strange, and C. L. Meyers, pp. 107-20. Cambridge, Mass.: American Schools of Oriental Research, 1981.

Smith, P., and L. K. Horwitz. "Culture, Environment and Disease: Palaeo-Anthropological Findings for the Southern Levant." In *Digging for Pathogenes,* edited by C. L. Greenblatt, pp. 201-39. Rehovot, Israel: Balaban Publishers, 1998.

Smith, P., L. K. Horwitz, and J. Zias. "Human Remains from the Iron Age Cemeteries at Akhziv: Part I; The Built Tomb from the Southern Cemetery." *Rivista di Studi Fenici* 18 (1990): 137-50.

Smith, P., and B. Peretz. "Hypoplasia and Health Status: A Comparison of Two Lifestyles." *Human Evolution* 6 (1986): 535-44.

Smith, P., and S. Tau. "Dental Pathology in the Period of the Roman Empire: A Comparison of Two Populations." *OSSA: International Journal of Skeletal Research* 5 (1979): 35-40.

Smith, W. R. *Lectures on the Religion of the Semites: Their Fundamental Institutions.* 3rd ed. London: A. & C. Black, 1927.

Soggin, J. A. *Israel in the Biblical Period: Institutions, Festivals, Ceremonies, Rituals.* Translated by J. Bowden. Edinburgh: T. & T. Clark, 2001.

Sperber, D. "Drought, Famine and Pestilence in Amoraic Palestine." *Journal of the Economic and Social History of the Orient* 17 (1974): 272-98.

Stadelman, W. J. "Chicken Eggs." In *The Cambridge World History of Food,* edited by K. F. Kiple and K. C. Ornelas, 1:499-508. Cambridge: Cambridge University Press, 2000.

Stager, L. E. "Ashkelon and the Archaeology of Destruction: Kislev 604 BCE." *Eretz Israel* 25 (1996): 61-74.

————. "First Fruits of Civilization." In *Palestine in the Bronze and Iron Age: Papers in Honour of Olga Tufnell,* edited by J. N. Tubb, pp. 172-87. London: Institute of Archaeology, 1985.

Steiner, R. C. *Stockmen from Tekoa, Sycomores from Sheba.* Catholic Biblical Quarterly, Monograph Series 36. Washington, D.C.: Catholic Biblical Association of America, 2003.

Stol, M. "Milk, Butter and Cheese." *Bulletin of Sumerian Agriculture* 7 (1993): 99-113.

Stuart-Macadam, P. L. "Nutritional Deficiency Diseases: A Survey of Scurvy, Rickets and Iron-Deficiency Anemia." In *Reconstruction of Life from the Skeleton,* edited by M. Y. Isçan and K. A. R. Kennedy, pp. 201-22. New York: Liss, 1989.

Taran, M. "Early Records of the Domestic Fowl in Ancient Judea." *Ibis* 117 (1975): 109-10.

Tchernov, E., and A. Drori. "Economic Patterns and Environmental Conditions at Hirbet El-Msas during the Early Iron Age." In *Ergebnisse der Ausgrabungen auf der Ḫirbet El-Mšaš (Ṭēl Māśoś) 1972-1975,* edited by V. Fritz and A. Kempinski, pp. 213-22. Wiesbaden: Otto Harrassowitz, 1983.

Thompson, T. L. *Early History of the Israelite People: From the Written and Archaeological Sources.* Studies in the History of the Ancient Near East 4. Leiden: Brill, 1992.

Unwin, T. *Wine and the Vine: An Historical Geography of Viticulture and the Wine Trade.* London: Routledge, 1991.

Van Neer, W., O. Lernau, R. Friedman, G. Mumford, J. Poblome, and M. Waelkens. "Fish Remains from Archaeological Sites as Indicators of Former Trade Connections in the Eastern Mediterranean." *Paléorient* 30 (2004): 101-48.

Walsh, C. E. *The Fruit of the Vine: Viticulture in Ancient Israel.* Harvard Semitic Monographs 60. Winona Lake, Ind.: Eisenbrauns, 2000.

Wapnish, P. "Archaeozoology: The Integration of Faunal Data with Biblical Archaeology." In *Biblical Archaeology Today, 1990: Proceedings of the Second International Congress on Biblical Archaeology,* edited by A. Biran and J. Aviram, pp. 426-42. Jerusalem: Israel Exploration Society, 1993.

————. "Archaeozoology at Tell Jemmeh: Taphonomy and Paleoeconomy in Historic Archaeology." Unpublished paper presented to the National Geographic Society, 1985.

Wapnish, P., and B. Hesse. "Faunal Remains from Tel Dan: Perspectives on Animal Production at a Village, Urban and Ritual Center." *Archaeozoologia* 4 (1991): 9-87.

————. "Pig Use and Abuse in the Ancient Levant: Ethnoreligious Boundary-Building with Swine." In *Ancestors for the Pigs: Pigs in Prehistory,* edited by

S. M. Nelson, pp. 123-36. MASCA Research Papers in Science and Archaeology. Philadelphia: University of Philadelphia Museum of Archaeology and Anthropology, 1998.

———. "Urbanization and the Organization of Animal Production at Tell Jemmeh in the Middle Bronze Age Levant." *Journal of Near Eastern Studies* 47 (1988): 81-94.

Watts, J. D. W. *Isaiah 1–33*. Word Biblical Commentary 24. Waco: Word, 1985.

Weinfeld, M. *Deuteronomy 1–11: A New Translation with Introduction and Commentary*. Anchor Bible 5. New York: Doubleday, 1991.

Wellhausen, J. *Prolegomena to the History of Israel*. Edinburgh: Adam and Charles Black, 1885.

West, D., M. Finnegan, R. W. Lane, and D. A. Kyasar. *Analysis of Faunal Remains Recovered from Tell Nimrin, Dead Sea Valley, Jordan*. http://www.case.edu/affil/nimrin/stdy/adaj/osteo/2000_0.pdf. Accessed 20 August 2007.

Weston Price Foundation. "Board of Directors." http://www.westonaprice.org/board.html. Accessed 27 September 2007.

White, K. D. *Roman Farming: Aspects of Greek and Roman Life*. Ithaca, N.Y.: Cornell University Press, 1970.

Whitelam, K. W. *The Invention of Ancient Israel: The Silencing of Palestinian History*. London: Routledge, 1996.

Wildberger, H. *Jesaja*. Biblischer Kommentar Altes Testament 10/3. Neukirchen-Vluyn: Neukirchener Verlag, 1982.

Wilkinson, J. *Jerusalem Pilgrims: Before the Crusades*. 2nd ed. Warminster: Aris and Phillips, 2002.

Zeder, M. A. *Feeding Cities: Specialized Animal Economy in the Ancient Near East*. Washington, D.C.: Smithsonian Institution Press, 1991.

———. "Pigs and Emergent Complexity in the Ancient Near East." In *Ancestors for the Pigs: Pigs in Prehistory*, edited by S. M. Nelson, pp. 109-22. Philadelphia: University of Philadelphia Museum of Archaeology and Anthropology, 1998.

Zertal, A. "The Cultivation and the Economy of Olives during the Iron Age I in the Hill Country of Manasseh." In *Olive Oil in Antiquity: Israel and Neighbouring Countries from the Neolithic to the Early Arab Period*, edited by D. Eitam and M. Heltzer, pp. 307-14. History of the Ancient Near East Studies 7. Padua: Sargon, 1996.

Ziegler, R., and J. Boessneck. "Tierrest der Eisenzeit II." In *Kinneret: Ergebnisse der Ausgrabungen auf dem Tell El-'Ormeam, See Gennesaret 1982-1985*, edited by V. Fritz, pp. 133-58. Wiesbaden: Harrassowitz, 1990.

Zohary, D., and M. Hopf. *Domestication of Plants in the Old World: The Origin and Spread of Cultivated Plants in West Asia, Europe, and the Nile Valley*. 2nd ed. Oxford: Clarendon, 1994.

Index of Modern Names

Index of Select Place Names, Authors, and Subjects

Index of Scripture References

28:48-40	56	4:28	21	**Proverbs**	
28:52-57	60	7:20	30	15:17	25
31:20	118n.14	10:2	40	27:26-27	35
		10:10	40	30:33	128n.15
Joshua		10:27	30		
5:6	7	17	57	**Isaiah**	
5:11	7, 21	17:12-13	24	1:22	22
19	84	19:6	21	5:1-7	22
		21	26	5:11-12	79
Judges				7:15	96, 146n.8
4:19	36	**2 Kings**		11:7	121n.19
5:25	35	4	26, 59	16:10	22
6:1-6	57	4:42	21	25:6	24
9:8-15	29	6	60	28:25	40, 121n.19
9:9	23	6:25	33	28:27	40
14	39	7:16	21	65:25	121n.19
19:19	121n.19	25:12	23		
				Jeremiah	
Ruth		**1 Chronicles**		4:9	28
1	57	12:40	29	7:18	21
2:14	23	14:14-15	30	11:5	118n.15
		27:28	24, 30	24	29
1 Samuel				32:22	118n.15
1:5	78	**2 Chronicles**		40:10	29
2	78	31:5	39	40:12	29
2:13	32			48:33	22
8:14	24	**Nehemiah**			
8:15	79	12:39	38	**Lamentations**	
10	100	13:16	38	2:20	60
14	39			4:10	60
17:17-18	128n.16	**Esther**	101		
17:18	35			**Ezekiel**	
25:18	29	**Job**		4:3	21
30:12	29	6:6	40	4:9	59, 119n.3, 121n.19
		21:24	36	5:10	60
2 Samuel		30:3-4	59	13:19	121n.16
5:23-24	30			16:13	24
16:1-2	29	**Psalms**		16:19	24
17:28	28	84:6	30	17:6-8	22
17:29	36	136:1	100	20	118n.17
		136:25	100	20:6	118n.15
1 Kings				20:15	3, 118n.15
4:22-23	78				

CPSIA information can be obtained
at www.ICGtesting.com
Printed in the USA
FFOW02n1347041217
43922801-42970FF